Scarecrow Studies
in Young Adult Literature
Series Editor: Patty Campbell

Scarecrow Studies in Young Adult Literature is intended to continue the body of critical writing established in Twayne's Young Adult Authors Series and to expand it beyond single-author studies to explorations of genres, multicultural writing, and controversial issues in YA reading. Many of the contributing authors of the series are among the leading scholars and critics of adolescent literature, and some are even YA novelists themselves.

The series is shaped by its editor, Patty Campbell, who is a renowned authority in the field, with a twenty-eight-year background as critic, lecturer, librarian, and teacher of young adult literature. In 1989 she was the winner of the American Library Association's Grolier Award for distinguished service to young adults and reading.

1. *What's So Scary about R.L. Stine?* by Patrick Jones, 1998.
2. *Ann Rinaldi: Historian and Storyteller,* by Jeanne M. McGlinn, 2000.

Ronald Phillip Rinaldi II as General Greene at the crossing of the Delaware.

Ann Rinaldi

Historian and Storyteller

Jeanne M. McGlinn

Scarecrow Studies in
Young Adult Literature, No. 2

The Scarecrow Press, Inc.
Lanham, Maryland, and London
2000

SCARECROW PRESS, INC.

Published in the United States of America
by Scarecrow Press, Inc.
4720 Boston Way, Lanham, Maryland 20706
www.scarecrowpress.com

4 Pleydell Gardens, Folkestone
Kent CT20 2DN, England

British Library Cataloguing in Publication Information Available

Library of Congress Cataloging-in-Publication Data

McGlinn, Jeanne Blain.
    Ann Rinaldi : historian and storyteller / Jeanne M. McGlinn.
        p.   cm. — (Scarecrow studies in young adult literature ; no. 2)
    Includes bibliographical references and index.
    ISBN 0-8108-3678-5 (alk. paper)
    1. Rinaldi, Ann—Criticism and interpretation. 2. Literature and history—
United States—History—20th century. 3. Young adult fiction, American—
History and criticism. 4. Historical fiction, American—History and criticism.
    I. Title. II. Scarecrow studies in young adult literature ; 2
  ⌐PS3568.I467 Z78 2000
    813'.54—dc21
                                                                    99-053130

Printed in the United States of America

∞™ The paper used in this publication meets the minimum requirements of
American National Standard for Information Sciences—Permanence of Paper
for Printed Library Materials, ANSI/NISO Z39.48–1992.

Contents

Editor's Foreword   vii
Preface   ix
Chronology   xi

1   Becoming a Writer of Historical Fiction   1
2   From Journalist to Fiction Writer   21
3   Coming of Age as Americans   39
4   Confronting Conflicting Values   53
5   Forging Individual Identity   65

    Afterword: Bringing History to Life   81
    Notes   83
    Bibliography   87
    Index   93
    About the Author   95

Editor's Foreword

As youth advocates, we know that young adults today are crying out for guidance in a risky world, for help with relationships, for spiritual and ethical direction, and most of all, for an answer to the most urgent teen question, "Who am I—and what am I going to do about it?" These are the big subjects that literature has always dealt with, and we are blessed with a growing body of splendid fiction for young adults that focuses on these questions. Some of the finest writing in America today is being done on the young adult level, and because the teen years are a complex and precarious time, this work gives rise to many controversial and difficult issues and problems. Contemporary young adult literature deserves serious critical attention—to analyze and report these issues, to present biocritical studies of leading writers, and to offer guidance in bringing teens and books together. Scarecrow Studies in Young Adult Literature is devoted to that task.

Developing an awareness of the past and its relevance to the present is a major task of adolescence, and so it is appropriate that the second volume in the series should focus on the leading writer of historical fiction for young adults, Ann Rinaldi. In these pages we find a vivid portrait of a woman in love with recreating American history and making it come alive for young people today. Future volumes in the series will continue to focus on single-author studies as well as the issues and controversies that make young adult fiction such a vital force in contemporary literature.

Patty Campbell
Series Editor

Preface

I first met Ann Rinaldi through her novel *Keep Smiling Through*, a fictionalized account of her World War II childhood. I read the book in one sitting, intrigued with the idealistic and vulnerable voice of Kay, the main character, who learns to "keep smiling through" even when things go wrong. In the note to this novel Rinaldi explains how she grew up during World War II in the midst of terrible fear and threat of danger but how she, like other children of this time, turned this anxiety into a drive to do her best in life. As I have gotten to know Ann Rinaldi better through her novels and through interviews and frequent telephone calls, my initial impressions about her talent, drive, and dedication to principle have been confirmed.

Rinaldi's talent is impressive. As she begins to write a new novel, she steeps herself in the particular period in time and emerges with vivid characters and an engaging story. And one can trust the accuracy of the historical milieu she has created. Rinaldi's study, where she writes her novels, is filled with history books, within easy reach when she wants to check accuracy or add details. She showed me several historical studies about the daily lives of women, which have helped her create the background for her characters. In recreating historical periods, Rinaldi holds herself to high standards. Many reviewers have noted the integrity of her historical research.

Rinaldi's drive is evident from her body of work, which consists of twenty-one years of writing for newspapers and twenty-five published novels, with more on the way. She is always working on a new idea. As we talked, it became clear that she has a lot of ideas—ideas that puzzle or challenge her—that she wants to explore. She is a natural storyteller who chooses the right way into a story and makes us care about her characters.

When I flew to New Jersey to meet Rinaldi, she graciously invited me to her home. She and her husband live in the small town of Somerville, a semirural area where grassy clearings spill over into woods. The resident deer population is rampant, as attested by chicken-wire fencing around Rinaldi's flower gardens. She took me through her home, showing me photos of her children, the book cover of *Time Enough for Drums*, in which her two children were used as models, the doll on her bed that her daughter gave her to replace Mary Frances, the doll Rinaldi gave up during the war like Kay in *Keep Smiling Through*. Each thing she pointed out had a history, a memory connected to it. In the family room are baskets of toys for her grandchildren, who often come to visit. Off the kitchen is Ron Rinaldi's workshop, where he worked on a remodeling project as Ann and I talked.

Rinaldi thinks of herself and her husband as fairly ordinary and normal. They have been married for thirty-eight years, living in the same community for most of that time. Yet looking back on their accomplishments—the family they have raised, the work they have done—she thinks what makes them interesting is how steady and committed they have been. But, she is quick to add, there is always more work to do.

Ann Rinaldi was always willing to talk with me, answer questions, and add information throughout the writing of this book, and I want her to know how much I valued her time. Others have assisted in the writing of this book. Patty Campbell, the series editor, provided clear and helpful guidance from the proposal stage throughout the production of the manuscript. John Mason at Scholastic and Rosemarie Rauch at Harcourt Brace were always willing to help and to answer my questions. The interlibrary loan and reference librarians at UNCA provided support and information. Students in the Adolescent Literature class at UNCA read and discussed several of Rinaldi's novels, and their interest and enthusiasm confirmed my own assessment of Rinaldi's writing. My thanks to all.

James McGlinn, my husband and colleague, provided invaluable assistance throughout the writing of this study. His thoughtful suggestions and steady encouragement were always helpful. My three children, Meghan, Ali, and Dan, were also a part of this work, encouraging and supporting me every step of the way.

Chronology

1934	Born 27 August in New York, N.Y., to Michael and Marcella (Dumarest) Feis.
1948	Attends high school in New Brunswick, N.J.
1960	Marries Ronald P. Rinaldi, chief lineman for Public Service Gas & Electric.
1969–1970	Writes for *Somerset Messenger Gazette*, Somerset, N.J.; writes self-syndicated column to eighteen daily papers in New York, New Jersey, and Pennsylvania.
1970–1991	Columnist, feature writer, and editorial writer for *The Trentonian*, Trenton, N.J.
1976	Assigned to write about the 200th anniversary celebration and reenactment of Washington's crossing the Delaware River; son Ron recruited to participate.
1978	Column "We Flew the Flag for Deborah Lipp" wins first place award given by the New Jersey Press Association.
1979	Reworks an untitled short story, which is bought by Walker, the first publisher who reads it.
1980	Publishes her first young adult (YA) novel, *Term Paper*.
1981	Writes for *The Trentonian* about the reenactment of the day Trenton learns of the Yorktown victory; decides to write a YA novel about the American Revolution.
1982	Publishes *Promises Are for Keeping*, sequel to *Term Paper*; completes the research and writing of *Time Enough for Drums*.
1985	*But in the Fall I'm Leaving* selected as a Notable Children's Trade Book in the Field of Social Studies by a joint committee of the National Council for Social Studies and the Children's Book Council.
1986	Publishes her first historical fiction novel for young adults, *Time Enough for Drums*, which is selected as an American Library Association Best Book for Young Adults.

1987   Receives the New Jersey Author's Award for *Time Enough for Drums*.

1988   *The Last Silk Dress* published and selected as an ALA Best Book for Young Adults.

1989   Column "Forget Spoiled Thirty-Somethings" wins first-place award given by the New Jersey Press Association.

1991   Wins the Daughters of the American Revolution's National History Award for her historical novels.

1992   *Wolf by the Ears* published and named an ALA Best Book for Young Adults, and later recognized as an ALA Best of the Best.

1993   *A Break with Charity* named an ALA Best Book for Young Adults.

1994   Publishes *A Stitch in Time*, first book in the "Quilt Trilogy," which is also named an American Bookseller Pick of the Lists; receives Pacific Northwest Library Association's Young Readers' Choice Award for *Wolf by the Ears*.

1995   Publishes *Broken Days*, second volume in the "Quilt Trilogy."

1996   Publishes *The Blue Door*, third volume in the "Quilt Trilogy"; *In My Father's House* (1993) receives Utah Young Adults' Book Award and also ALA Best Book for Young Adults and IRA/CBC Young Adult Choice awards.

1997   *An Acquaintance with Darkness* named an ALA Best Book for Young Adults and a New York Public Library Book for the Teen Age; *The Second Bend in the River* published and chosen as an American Bookseller Pick of the Lists.

1998   *Mine Eyes Have Seen* and *Cast Two Shadows* are published.

1999   *My Heart Is on the Ground* (part of the Dear America series), *The Coffin Quilt*, and *Amelia's War* are published.

2000   *The Journal of Jasper Jonathan Pierce, a Pilgrim Boy, Plimoth Plantation, 1620*, part of the *My Name Is America* series, is scheduled to be published.

Becoming a Writer of Historical Fiction

*C*hristmas day, 1976. Ann Rinaldi stands on the banks of the Delaware River, watching a reenactment of Washington's crossing. Two hundred years earlier, on the night of December 25, 1776, General George Washington crossed the Delaware River in a blinding snowstorm with 2,400 colonial troops, horses, and artillery. He planned to attack the British and Hessians in the town of Trenton, New Jersey. The crossing took until four o'clock in the morning because of the weather, but when the Continental Army made their surprise attack, the Hessians were routed, surrendering after an hour. Nearly 1,000 were taken prisoner with only six wounded in Washington's army. This victory came at an important point for the Continental Army, which had suffered steady losses to the larger, more heavily armed, and better trained British forces. Before the battle even Washington thought the end was near, but he did not back down.

This act of courage and daring on the part of Washington and his soldiers is one of the cultural icons of the United States. For most Americans, the image comes from a famous painting. In 1851 Emanuel Leutze portrayed the moment of setting out across the river with Washington standing upright at the helm of a boat that flounders in icy waters.[1] The arrangement of the figures, the light breaking through the clouds, the Stars and Stripes blowing back in the wind—all contribute to the drama of the moment and Leutze's intention to teach a lesson about heroic courage.

Ann Rinaldi was a columnist for *The Trentonian* in 1976 when her editor, Emil Slaboda, assigned her to interview the man playing Washington in the annual reenactment of the crossing. During the interview, Rinaldi learned that boys were needed to play roles and agreed to ask her son, Ron, who was fourteen, if he wanted to join in. This was the beginning of his fascination with history. Rinaldi recalls how Ron "fell in love with the whole thing."[2] That summer he and his sister Marcella, who was twelve, worked as volunteers at the visitors' center on the Pennsylvania side of the Delaware. Ron started collecting antique uniforms and weapons to outfit himself and joined a local reenactment group. By 1978 Rinaldi, her husband, and her daughter Marcella were all traveling to reenactments. Rinaldi credits her son's enthusiasm and the reenactments with interesting her in becoming a writer of historical fiction. "He dragged us into it. . . . He got bitten by the history bug and passed the disease to me."[3] Since 1976, no matter how cold or snowy the weather, Rinaldi and her family continue to attend the crossing of the Delaware. Ronald Rinaldi takes the part of a soldier and Ron, their son, now plays the role of General Greene and takes along his own son.

In the late 1970s, Rinaldi and her family joined several local groups, like the Egg Harbor Guard and the Bergen County Militia, that actually existed during the American Revolution. Local reenactment groups are under the umbrella of the Brigade of the American Revolution, which requires that each group be thoroughly researched and authentic before it is reactivated. In such groups, members decide on their own specialties. For example, a woman might become an expert in candle-dipping and then demonstrate this skill, or a man might portray a doctor and for the role would acquire the instruments used at that time. Rinaldi has played the role of a soldier's wife and performed the women's duties of making clothes and cooking food. Everything has to be an accurate re-creation of life in the eighteenth century. Rinaldi recalls cooking over a campfire the kind of food that would have been eaten in the eighteenth century. Pies were made in cast-iron pots buried in the ashes. Soups and stews were cooked on tripods. Chicken was cooked on a spit. She says, "We were living history. People were experts. You could talk to these people and your research was right in front of you . . . you could go up to a person and ask who he was and write it down and you had it." Rinaldi absorbed information about what people were doing, how they were acting, how they dressed, what equipment they used—an engaging way to learn history.

Throughout the bicentennial years, 1978–1986, Rinaldi and her family followed the progress of the American Revolution by traveling to the towns and battlefields of the war, across all thirteen of the original colonies and Ohio—from Trenton to Sackets Harbor, New York; through small New Jersey towns; and to Georgia for the Siege of Savannah in 1979. Rinaldi recalls, "My son dragged us to every battlefield, monument, fort, and battleground, north and south, from Saratoga to Yorktown. I began to see the history of my country as it was, from the bottom up . . . instead of out of a history book" (*SATA*, vol. 51, 151). At Yorktown, Virginia, in 1981 Rinaldi "saw" the surrender of the British army to the Americans. Ron was in college by then and his sister was seventeen when they participated in this reenactment, living in the field for three days. Rinaldi describes this experience in the note to *In My Father's House*, "Then I witnessed, recreated, the terrible silence in the presence of so many assembled souls, 'no trumpet, no drumroll, no cheers' from any Americans up and down the line, while all held their breath as the British lay down their colors and their arms."[4]

Reenactment experiences have been Rinaldi's school of history. She says, "I learned my history hands-on, making the clothes of the eighteenth century, cooking the food, learning the songs, dances, philosophy, lifestyle." She draws on these details to create the texture and nuances of daily life in her novels. They also give her insight into the feelings of the people of the times. When writing *In My Father's House* (1993), Rinaldi drew on her experiences at Yorktown to create the emotional scene of the surrender from a different war, of the Confederate Army at Appomattox. She says, "I was fortunate to have been at that reenactment of the surrender of the British to the Americans. And like Oscie [the main character of the novel] I shall never forget it as long I live. All I had to do to recreate the incredible sense of history was to change the uniforms and the era. Surely the emotions when the South surrendered to the North must have been similar" (*House*, 311).

Rinaldi decided to write an historical novel in 1981 after participating in the surrender at Yorktown. While she was at the encampment, she says she suddenly had a sense of déjà vu—"I've been here before." She says, "I said to myself: 'Ann, why are you doing this; you've done this all once before.'" When she got home, she was assigned by her editor at *The Trentonian* to cover the reenactment of the day Trenton learned of the Yorktown victory. "I realized I was going to write a young adult novel on the American Revolution. A good one. Not one utilizing all the myths and the famous figures" (*SATA*, vol. 51, 151). It took about one year for Rinaldi to complete the research and writing of *Time Enough for Drums*, which describes conditions in Trenton as Tories and Rebels figure out their loyalties and deal with British and Hessian occupation.

However, the novel was not published until 1986; ten publishers rejected it because they didn't think children would read about history. Rinaldi knew they were wrong. She had been to many reenactments and had seen how interested children were in history, plus she had the experience of her own children. Four years went by before Holiday House, which had already published one of her realistic young adult novels and had her under contract for another, decided to give the historical novel a try. Kate Briggs, co-owner of Holiday House, was a member of the International Reading Association, which was calling for more literature-based instruction and the use of literature to teach content. She encouraged Rinaldi's editor at Holiday House, Margery Cuyler, to call Rinaldi and tell her to set aside her current project and revise her historical novel. Rinaldi says, "It's been nothing but history ever since." This first novel opened up the flood of her imagination and love of history, and one novel has led to another. These are the novels she wants to write: "I went against the grain of what everybody told me, but then, that's what I did in my lifetime, too" (*SATA*, vol. 51, 151). Today most major juvenile publishers have a line of historical books for girls. Rinaldi is proud to have helped to pioneer this development in young adult literature.

GETTING IDEAS FOR HISTORICAL NOVELS

Ideas are everything for a writer of historical fiction, and Rinaldi is always alert for the story, character, or event that may spark her next novel. Ideas come to her in two ways: through research and reading lots of books about history and through everyday experiences.

Rinaldi reads extensively as she prepares to write a novel, and this process often sparks new, totally unexpected ideas. As she's reading, pulling books off the shelves, she'll come across something she wasn't even looking for and suddenly a new idea will occur to her. Recently when she was doing research for another novel, she came across a book on West Virginia and Kentucky and the myths and folklore about the feuds between the Hatfields and McCoys. Suddenly, she says, "It all came together for me." She connected the historical feuding families with violent militia and hate groups of today and decided to write a book about the Hatfields and McCoys, which became *The Coffin Quilt*, one of her latest novels.

Rinaldi does all her own research. She doesn't understand how some writers hire another person to do it for them. Without the reading and research, Rinaldi doesn't think she would make new discoveries or create the characters to tell her stories. For example, when she was re-creating the Boston Massacre, she needed a protagonist. While reading *The Book of Abigail and John, Selected Letters of the Adams Family, 1762–1784*, Rinaldi came across a letter in which John Adams describes his search to find the right girl to serve as a maid to the family. He mentions, "Another Girl, one Rachel Marsh, has been recommended to me as a clever Girl and a neat one and one that wants a Place."[5] From this brief hint, Rinaldi created the main character, emphasizing the idea that she is a person who desires to find "a place" in the world.[6]

But inspiration also comes from everyday experiences. Her idea to write about Harriet Hemings in *Wolf by the Ears* (1991) started when she was reading a book about the private life of Thomas Jefferson. But Rinaldi says her real reason for writing the book "had nothing to do with history." It came about because of a unique set of circumstances. Rinaldi was working for *The Trentonian* when a middle-aged man appeared at the newspaper office, claiming to be the Lindbergh baby. During this time in New Jersey, conspiracy theories had developed around this famous case to account for the disappearance of the baby. One of these theories maintained that the baby was not really killed; rather he was in a car accident with his mother, suffered some type of head trauma, and was sent away by the family. People claiming to be the Lindbergh baby try to prove their identity through this theory. Also Anna Hauptmann, the wife of the man executed for kidnapping and killing the Lindbergh baby, lived into her nineties, and from time to time she would present new evidence to clear her husband's name. When she did, the state police in Trenton would hold a news conference. Rinaldi says she met three "Lindbergh babies" while she was a newspaper columnist. So when this particular man showed up at Rinaldi's desk, she began to think, "How sad to spend your whole life and everything you had . . . trying to prove you are the son or daughter of this important man and only desiring to be acknowledged." She says, "That idea stayed with me and I said if I could find somebody in history I would tell this story." This idea in the back of her mind led Rinaldi eventually to Harriet Hemings, a slave who believes herself to be Jefferson's daughter. Rinaldi says, "This shows that books do not come at us all in a piece—one thing stays with you—how sad, how terrible, how awful, or there's a puzzle you have to solve and you want to look for a way to solve it." So many of Rinaldi's ideas come to her in unexpected ways, but once she has an idea, her "need to know,"[7] her desire to solve the puzzle, takes over and leads to extensive research.

DOING THE RESEARCH AND
PREPARING TO WRITE AN HISTORICAL NOVEL

Rinaldi reads both primary and secondary sources, everything about the time, place, culture, and daily life. She tries to immerse herself in the history from every possible side. Primary documents include contemporary accounts of events, letters, and town records. For example, in one of her most recent novels, *My Heart Is on the Ground*, Rinaldi used the Carlisle Indian Industrial School newspaper, *Eadle keatah toh*, or *The Morning Star*, as the source of some of the events depicted in the novel.[8]

Students of Native American history can visit a home page describing the Carlisle Indian Industrial School history, which has links to one of the school's newsletters, "The Indian Helper." This site has been prepared by Barbara Landis, a researcher and library assistant of the Cumberland County Historical Society in Carlisle, Pennsylvania, where Carlisle Indian School newspapers are housed (http://www.home.epix.net/~landis/histry.html). Researchers can also follow a link to "Primary Sources," prepared by Landis and Genevieve Bell, another researcher who has been developing a database of student folders in "Record Group 75, File 1327" at the National Archives (http://home.epix.net/~landis/primary.html).

Landis and Bell warn that Indian School newspapers are "highly propagandistic. They were written by Indian School students as part of their Printing Training, under the heavy editorial eye of the school administrators, especially the founding father, Richard Henry Pratt, whose tenure at Carlisle covered the period from 1879 until his dismissal in 1904."[9] They often contained articles describing the benefits of assimilation. Rinaldi echoes this caution in the historical note to the novel, saying that school newspapers were "used by Captain Pratt as a private platform from which to spread his ideas about teaching" (*Heart*, 179). Also, the names of the papers changed frequently, making them difficult to track. *Eadle keatah toh* was published between April 1880 and March 1882; its name was then changed to *Red Man* and *Red Man & Helper*. *Morning Star* was published monthly between April 1882 and December 1887, according to Landis and Bell.

For Rinaldi the research is ongoing. Before she begins to write, she does character profiles, but these are not lengthy. She prefers to keep her research open. She continues to refer to books and resources even after she begins to write. She says, "Sometimes in writing a page, I have to stop two times to look something up." Rinaldi doesn't use dialect for the most part, but she creates vocabulary lists of words characters would use, given their ages and the time and place. Again in *My Heart Is on the Ground*, Rinaldi spent some time creating an authentic word list for a Sioux girl who is just learning English. She decided to show the girl's increasing fluency by having her use a limited vocabulary that develops during the course of the novel. Rinaldi also invented a plausible reason why Nannie Little Rose, a twelve-year-old Lakota Sioux girl, knows some English. She has learned from her friend, Red Road, who is a member of her tribe and wife of Charles Tackett, a white trader. So Little Rose is given a diary to write because "Teacher tells it that I know some English, that she is much proud of me, but wants be more proud. And if I do this thing I can learn better the English words and soon be A-Friend-to-Go-Between-Us, like Red Road" (*Heart*, 3).

Debbie Reese and other reviewers have been highly critical of Rinaldi's way of showing Nannie's rapid language development. Reese and others posted a lengthy review of *My Heart Is on the Ground* to Child_Lit, an on-line discussion group devoted to theory and criticism of children's literature, April 12, 1999, and a Web board at the National Council of Social Studies, April 12, 1999. A longer version of the review was posted to Oyate, a web-site devoted to issues of Native Americans, "working to see that our lives and histories are portrayed honestly, and so that all people will know our stories belong to us" (http://www.oyate.org). *Multicultural Review* also published the review essay.[10] Reviewers criticize the authenticity of Nannie's language. "Throughout, Rinaldi uses stereotyped language to express Lakota (or 'Indian') speech and thought patterns."[11] They contend she uses too many compound words to suggest Indian speech patterns, which is not warranted because self-sufficient Lakota words exist for certain concepts. Reviewers for *Booklist* and *Kirkus Reviews* (only several reviews of this novel have appeared in press by the summer of 1999) do not find Nannie's language development problematic. Stephanie Zvirin in *Booklist*[12] says that Nannie's broken English grows realistically "more polished as the story continues." *Kirkus Reviews* indicates that Nannie's language development parallels her psychological state, "Beginning with slow, laboring words that lead first to ghastly realization, and then to mature understanding."[13] Disagreement about Nannie's language is one of several controversies that have surrounded the publication of this novel.

VISITS TO HISTORICAL SITES

Rinaldi often visits historic sites to get information. She had been to Morristown National Historical Park and the Wick House, which are the setting for *A Ride into the Morning* (1991), many times before the idea of doing a story on the legend of Tempe Wick was suggested to her by her literary agent, Joanna Cole. For *In My Father's House*, Rinaldi visited three historic sites: Manassas, Charlottesville, and Appomattox Court House. While on a research trip to western Maryland in November 1996 for another book, Rinaldi met John Frye, curator of the Western Maryland Room at the

Washington County Free Library in Hagerstown, Maryland, and Mary K. Baykan, director of the library. They took her on a tour of the area, which included the Kennedy Farm where John Brown lived with his Provisional Army for three months in the summer of 1859. Rinaldi writes, "When I saw that log cabin sitting on that rise in the foothills of western Maryland and read the marker . . . then found out about fifteen-year-old Annie Brown being a part of this dramatic moment in our history, I knew I had a story."[14]

For *My Heart Is on the Ground* Rinaldi made two trips to the Carlisle Indian Industrial School in Carlisle, Pennsylvania, which was started in 1879 by Captain Richard Henry Pratt, where American Indians were sent to be "Americanized." Rinaldi describes visiting the school cemetery, "with dozens of white headstones bearing the names of the Native American children from all tribes who had died while at the school. The names, with the tribes inscribed underneath, were so lyrical that they leapt out at me and took on instant personalities. Although many of these children attended Carlisle at dates later than that of my story, I used some of their names for classmates of Nannie Little Rose. In one respect I hoped to bring them alive again and show their plight and their accomplishments to young readers today" (*Heart*, 195–196). Native children were given "new" names when they entered the school. Rinaldi describes this traumatic experience for Little Rose. She questions her teacher's pronouncement that her real name ties her to a "savage past" and becomes angry. Little Rose gives in, but says to herself, "I will never forget my past" (*Heart*, 50).

The Oyate reviewers criticize Rinaldi's "appropriation" of Native children's names as a sign of lack of respect for the children and the tragedy of their experiences (*Oyate*, 8) because the full implications of this action don't come out clearly in the novel. The Oyate reviewers say, "In taking away the linguistic Indian name—which had been a source of strength, cultural pride, and psychic identity—and making the 'new' names very common, written everywhere, used again and again, they [teachers and administrators of the boarding schools] in effect erased all spiritual aspects of the children's identities" (*Oyate*, 5). There is also a strong disagreement about whether it is appropriate to use real names in a story. The Scholastic Press editor of the Dear America series cites Louise Erdrich's use of real people's names from census records in *Birchbark House* (Hyperion 1999) as a way to honor and give life to a person who lived long ago (April 23, 1999) (http://www.scils.rutgers.edu/childlit/april99/0217.html). Debbie Reese contends that there is an essential difference between the context of the two stories. She says, "If the editorial staff and Ms. Rinaldi spend some time with Native people, talking with them firsthand, listening to their stories and feelings about boarding schools, you [the publisher] may gain some insight and understanding as to why this use of names is so problematic for us" (April 24, 1999) (http://www.scils.rutgers.edu/childlit/april99.0151.html). This controversy suggests the issues facing writers of historical fiction, especially when they come from a different cultural orientation than the people they are depicting.

Rinaldi has also researched the role of women in American history. She says, "Usually history is about dates, battles, and politics," and women are often left out. Recently there has been excellent research about women that helps to give a fuller account of their lives. Rinaldi cites many of these books in bibliographies at the end of each novel. She also keeps these books available in the study where she writes. If she wants to check a particular detail about the lives of women, Rinaldi draws on this body of current historical research. She is constantly looking for resources that tell her about daily life and the home in the past; these are the details that create the authentic setting and atmosphere of her novels. In all of her novels so far, Rinaldi tells her stories through female adolescent characters. Often they display courage, make important decisions, and act in ways that have an impact on the outcome of events. These are not weak or passive girls. But Rinaldi says, "I'm not writing solely to project a female point of view. I feel comfortable at the present moment writing from a young girl's point of view; however, I always have very strong supporting roles for young men and boys in my books." Rinaldi uses her research to create an authentic depiction of the ways men and women interacted in the historical periods in her novels.

Research and site visits are important, but Rinaldi also has a "resident expert" available, her son Ron. She checks the historical accuracy of her research with Ron, who has a Master's in history and has done Ph.D. graduate work. In almost every one of her novels, she cites her debt to his knowledge and his extensive library of American and military history. To this day, Rinaldi continues to ask him to identify and critique resources. She can take questions to him and discuss ideas. She says, "I might not have been able to write the history novels without Ron's support."

Even though Rinaldi does thorough research, there is always the possibility that new information may come to light even while she is writing a novel. This happened when she was telling the story of Wilmer McLean, whose two homes turned out to be the site of two key events in the Civil War, the Battle of Manassas and the Surrender at Appomattox. Just as Rinaldi was working with the final copyediting of *In My Father's House,* she learned about new research on McLean. She was able to include some of this new information in the manuscript before it was sent to the publisher. But some things couldn't be changed without changing the whole plot, which is impossible in the last stages before the novel is published. For example, Rinaldi has Maria Mason, one of McLean's stepdaughters, marrying Michah Stevens, a Yankee from Marietta, Ohio, when in fact she married Philip Lee. Rinaldi cites this discrepancy in her note to this novel, "to show how I improvised for the sake of plot, when I ran into dead ends in history" (*House*, 306–307). She considers the sudden appearance of new information as one of the pitfalls for historical novelists. At the same time, she sees this as a sign that historical study is alive and well. Rinaldi writes, "Such instances show that history, what we may regard as a 'dead' subject not worth bothering with, is constantly being revived and rejuvenated with the emergence of newly found letters, court records, or diaries, some discovered in people's attics, and others there for the scholar who bothers to track them down in various places" (*House*, 307).

Historical research and accuracy are essential, but the historical novelist must also put the facts together to tell a compelling story. When the facts fail, the novelist uses her imagination to unravel the puzzle. Rinaldi did this in *The Last Silk Dress* (1988), for example, when she couldn't find research that verified that the Confederacy had its own reconnaissance balloon for spying on troop movements. Rinaldi decided "that if it [the existence of the balloon] was fiction I would take the tale one step further and create a story of how such a silk dress balloon might have come into being."[15] When the historical record is silent about people's motives, the novelist invents the reasons why people act as they do. Rinaldi says, "All historical novelists have to invent much of the motivation of their characters in order to take them from one historically accurate event to the next" (*House*, 307). Therefore, when there is controversy, such as that over the role of Peggy Shippen, wife of Benedict Arnold, in urging him to turn traitor, "historical novelists have to come down on one side or the other. We novelists take risks when we make such decisions."[16]

THE "QUILT TRILOGY":
APPLYING IMAGINATION TO THE FACTS OF HISTORY

Rinaldi usually doesn't write about heroes. Mainly, she tells stories of common people living during historical times. This side of her writing is best demonstrated by the three volumes of the "Quilt Trilogy"—*A Stitch in Time*, *Broken Days*, and *The Blue Door*—written between 1994 and 1996. Rinaldi describes these novels as examples of what an historical novelist does best—apply imagination to the facts of history. Rinaldi takes "data uninteresting to the lay person and fill[s] in the dots between the facts with colorful characters and their motivation."[17]

Rinaldi describes her process of combining facts and imagination to create these three novels in the note to *A Stitch in Time*. She started with an idea "to write about a family that gets torn apart, seemingly by events outside the home, but actually by dark undercurrents from within, undercurrents that reach out from the past . . ."(*Stitch*, 293). She also wanted to symbolize what happens to the family through an object. She chose a quilt, having worked on quilts and knowing how they are often passed from one generation to the next and are sewn and restored by different persons. The quilt could be divided between three sisters, the main characters in the series, and so serve to identify their descendants over the years. Having or not having a piece of the quilt becomes an issue in each novel, leading to conflict when the piece is stolen or lost and a member of the family cannot prove her identity. In the end the restoration of the quilt pieces leads to the resolution of the family conflict.

Having decided to use the quilt as the key object, Rinaldi wanted to choose a location that had to do with the manufacture of fabric. Reading about the Lowell mills, Rinaldi "learned that one of the first attempts at manufacturing cotton in America was in Beverly, Massachusetts, near Salem" (*Stitch*, 294). This led her to choose Salem. Now she had the idea, the object that would tie the three novels together, and the location. She conducted extensive research on Salem during the Revolutionary War and after. She read about "ships, trade routes, privateers, counting houses, the lives of sea captains and the merchants who backed them financially" (*Stitch*, 295). She also had the idea that one of the sisters would be captured by the Indians, so she has members of the family traveling west to the Ohio Territory. From her research, Rinaldi creates the complicated canvas against which her characters live and act. In the end the trilogy includes Salem, its shipping and complex merchant culture; the struggle for control of shipping lanes and trade routes, particularly between Great Britain and America, which resulted in the War of 1812; the expansion westward and the warfare between Indians and Whites; pre-Civil War southern plantation culture; and the growth of textile manufacturing and the development of the factory system in New England. In fact the growth and development of the textile industry moves from off-center in the first novel to the focus in the last two novels. The second novel, *Broken Days*, is set in 1812 because "this was the time of the second phase in the development of cotton mills in New England" (*Days*, 264). In 1814 Nathaniel Chelmsford, patriarch of the family, starts a factory in Waltham,

Massachusetts, with the first power loom (*Days*, 264). In the third novel, *The Blue Door*, set in 1841, the southern planters turn to the mills of the North to buy and manufacture their raw cotton. The main character, Amanda Videau, great granddaughter of Nathaniel Chelmsford, is sent North to get a better price for her father's cotton, and through a series of mishaps, ends up working in his mill and fighting to improve conditions for the "mill girls." Rinaldi says she chose 1841 because "it was the year of the first stirrings of the labor movement in America, the year the girls in Lowell were circulating their ten-hour petition."[18]

Rinaldi acknowledges that historical fiction writers do not stop with the facts. They use facts to create their stories; they build on the facts through imagination; they explore the facts to see what ideas emerge. In each novel she carefully points out what is fact and what is fiction in the author's note. In this trilogy all the characters are fictional (*Stitch*, 296), with the exception of several minor characters in each book. Reverend William Bentley, "one of Salem's most notable and compassionate pastors," was based on information from his own diary (*Stitch*, 299). The father of Richard Lander, Peter Lander, did exist; he commanded a ship out of Salem. There was also a Captain William Burnaby, a commander of a British warship in 1775, but Rinaldi created the story of his relationship with Chelmsford's wife and gave him a son, Cabot. *In Broken Days*, there are several real people, like Nathaniel Hawthorne as a boy and Sarah Bryant, mother of the poet William Cullen Bryant. But this doesn't mean the fictionalized characters are not true. Usually they are "composites," based on real persons who lived at the time. For example, Nathaniel Chelmsford is based on several men involved in the textile industry, including "Francis Cabot Lowell, who was one of the founders of the Lowell mills" (*Stitch*, 297). Louis Gaudineer, who travels west as a militiaman and searches for Thankful Chelmsford when she is taken captive, is based on many men "like him who went west to try to keep peace between the settlers and the Indians" (*Stitch*, 297). In the note to *Broken Days*, Rinaldi says Gaudineer is "based on Indian Agent Captain William Wells. . . . I have Louis, like Wells, preventing a massacre at Fort Wayne, being adopted by the Miamis, and then killed by Indians at Fort Dearborn" (*Days*, 266). In *The Blue Door*, Rinaldi notes, "With the exception of Lucy Larcom, Lizzy Turner, Clementine Averill, and Harriot Curtis, who actually worked in the mills and were activists at this time, just about everyone else in the book is made up" (*Blue Door*, 267). But again the fictional characters "have roles and motivations rooted in history" (*Blue Door*, 267).

The trilogy follows the mostly fictional Chelmsford family from 1788 to 1841. In 1788 the narrator Hannah is seventeen. She is the family peacekeeper, trying to compensate for her father's harsh treatment of her siblings. Chelmsford, always a domineering person, nurses secret anger over his suspicion that Cabot is not his son. His wife, now dead, had an affair with a British captain, and Chelmsford has never forgiven her. He doesn't allow her name to be mentioned in the family and he belittles Cabot. His favorite is Thankful, who manipulates her position as favored daughter to get her own way. Chelmsford, Lawrence (his oldest son), and Thankful journey to the western territory so he can set up trading posts, and when Thankful is captured by the Indians, Chelmsford blames everyone except himself. He also disowns his other daughter, Abigail, who elopes with Captain Nate Videau against her father's wishes. Chelmsford turns all his energies to the establishment of the first mill in Beverly, getting Hannah to help him improve living conditions for the mill girls. He also allows her to raise the half-Indian daughter of Louis Gaudineer, who has promised to continue the search for Thankful.

In *Broken Days*, Hannah is thirty-nine, and the fourteen-year-old narrator, Ebie, is her brother Cabot's child. Walking Breeze, Thankful's child, is told by her dying mother to return to the family home in Salem and given a piece of quilt to "tell them who you are" (*Days,* 12). Ebie steals the quilt piece because she fears being dispossessed "as the only grandchild Grandfather will acknowledge in this family" (*Days,* 31). In time, Ebie learns the truth about her father's illegitimate birth and realizes that she isn't really Chelmsford's granddaughter. Meanwhile Walking Breeze, Americanized as Nancy, learns about making cloth and begins to supervise the dyeing of fabric at the mill. In the end, Ebie has the courage to reveal her lie and the Shawnee daughter of Thankful is reunited with the family.

In *The Blue Door*, the last novel of the trilogy, the narrator is Amanda Videau, granddaughter of Abigail Chelmsford Videau. Amanda is given a piece of quilt to identify her to her great grandfather and so that this part of the quilt can "be pieced together with the rest of it" (*Blue Door,* 56). On the journey North, Amanda meets Elinora Rhordan, a woman who is running away from her abusive husband and who works in the mill of her great grandfather in Lowell. Amanda loses her quilt piece when the boilers on board the steamboat explode and she is thrown into the waters of Long Island Sound. To protect Elinora she takes on the identity of her sister Clara who has been killed in the accident and ends up working in the weaving room. "They . . . set me to threading shuttles. They gave me a loom. They had more than enough to give. The room was filled with looms. And girls. All sizes of girls who moved about tending two or more machines" (*Blue Door,* 138). Amanda learns about the terrible conditions of this backbreaking work firsthand and is told that the girls are organizing to demand better working conditions. They are circulating a petition to reduce their workday from thirteen to ten hours, but most of the girls are afraid to sign because they fear they will be dismissed from the factory. This is how Amanda meets her cousin, Nancy/Walking Breeze Chelmsford. Nancy is well respected because she runs the dyeing room and creates designs for the prints. Amanda gives her a design of a bird, taken from a letter to her grandmother, in exchange for Nancy's support on the petition. Amanda also tells her story to Nancy, who helps her meet Chelmsford and eventually Ebie, just as Amanda returns to her home in the South. The three pieces of the quilt are collected, ready for the women to piece together "just like Aunt Hannah, Aunt Abigail, and Aunt Thankful would have done" (*Blue Door*, 258). By creating these layers of connections through several generations and showing what happens to the teenage characters as they mature into adulthood and old age, Rinaldi shows how historical events are really human events and how they are all interrelated. She says, "Everything we do in life affects those around us and those who follow us" (*Blue Door*, 265). She also gives her readers "a sense of *having lived all those years with my characters, seen them grow up, affect each other, and pass on*" (*Blue Door*, 266).

MEETING NEW CHALLENGES
IN *MY HEART IS ON THE GROUND*

My Heart Is on the Ground (1999), part of the Dear America series, is one of Rinaldi's latest novels. It is a fictional diary of Nannie Little Rose, daughter of the Lakota Sioux chief White Thunder, who like other Native American children is recruited by Captain Richard Henry Pratt, founder of the Carlisle Indian School, in the fall of 1879. Pratt had developed a strong assimilationist philosophy while in charge of Fort Marion Prison in St. Augustine, Florida, where warriors from Cheyenne, Kiowa, Comanche, and Caddo Nations were imprisoned. Pratt sought resources from the federal government and private philanthropists to found a school where Native children would be educated to function in the white world.[19] Little Rose describes how this process required erasing Native identity. During the first days at the school, her Indian clothing is taken away and she is given "citizens' clothing," or what white people wear. Her hair is cut, going against all her cultural traditions. She is forced to choose a new English name and is not allowed to speak in her native language. Everything is done to make the children forget their identity, tribe, and past traditions. Nannie Little Rose questions why this is necessary, knowing that Indians are not all the same, just as not all Indians are at war with the whites.

Little Rose promises herself that she will hold onto her identity and her past. For her this means being true to Lakota values. Everything she does at the school, her efforts to excel in learning, are grounded in her desire to do an act of bravery that befits a Lakota Sioux girl. At the beginning of her diary, Nannie Little Rose says, "I am frightened much to do this thing. I am about a hundred miles lost at the start. But I will keep in my path and not let it run away from me. . . . I was sent here to do a brave act for my people. I want to make like much smart for my teacher" (*Heart*, 4). Little Rose looks for the spirit helper who will help her identify a brave deed and eventually realizes that it is a kitchen mouse. Little Rose says, "What have I done to earn a spirit helper? Nothing. Yet the little mouse came and spoke to me in my dream. I am grateful for him" (*Heart*, 85). He tells her "part of the bravery is in knowing when I am needed. In stepping forth at the right time" (*Heart*, 86). Little Rose decides she has to help her friend, Pretty Eagle, who is encouraging the other children and reminding them of their Indian traditions and values. She thinks this is her "vision," her destiny, but in time she discovers that there is other work for her, too. Later, Little Rose is unable to save Pretty Eagle when she goes into a deep trance and appears to be dead. Although Little Rose experiences deep sadness, she learns the honor of forgiving an enemy, Belle Rain Water, the girl she blames for Pretty Eagle's death. Her mouse spirit helper tells Little Rose that "sometimes it is more honorable to forgive your enemy than to stay angry" (*Heart*, 155). When she sees Pretty Eagle's eyes in Belle's, Little Rose has her sign, and she asks Belle Rain Water's help to rescue her brother who is trying to come back to the school after finding he no longer fits on the reservation. Little Rose also decides to become a teacher so she can return to the reservation and teach other children. Everything Little Rose does, according to the story, is actually a fulfillment of her Indian identity. She learns white ways, but not by denying who she is.

Rinaldi faced several technical and artistic puzzles with this novel. As mentioned earlier, she immediately realized that she had to make it plausible that Little Rose could write a diary and that her usage and facility with English would increase over time. Rinaldi handles this challenge by first giving Little Rose the relationship with Red Road, which explains why she knows some English words. Then, too, Little Rose writes the diary in order to improve her use of language, so this provides her motivation for writing in the first place. Little Rose talks with her teacher about grammar, tense changes, and the way English words have multiple meanings. Little Rose even corrects her grammar as her knowledge grows. The change from more limited usage to more complex vocabulary and syntax happens in a seamless and unobtrusive way. The reader notices fewer grammatical changes but still hears Little Rose's earlier speech patterns. Her unique voice comes through in the story.

Facing the challenge of writing about another culture, Rinaldi visited Carlisle and immersed herself in its history. Assimilating her experiences and reading, Rinaldi formed a picture of what happened when children were brought to boarding schools like Carlisle—how some children adjusted whereas others suffered extreme trauma, how for some the school was a way to learn new vocations but for others the school created a barrier between them and their tribal communities. Then Rinaldi let readers live through these days with Little Rose, experiencing her adjustments and reactions, limiting everything to her point of view. Little Rose does not see the issues of her situation in all their complexity.

Little Rose is disoriented and frightened in an alien environment. She fears punishment and embarrassment, which is compounded because she doesn't even know the mistakes that may get her in trouble. Somehow Little Rose adjusts—maybe because of her relationship with Red Road, an older woman and friend who accompanies the children, or because she wants to please her teachers. Nannie also has successes that other children would not have had. She already knows a bit of English and acts as a translator, she gets a prize for her sewing, and she enjoys the company of her special friend, Lucy Pretty Eagle, who arrives at the school. Her brother Whiteshield reacts differently, at first rebelling and getting in trouble, and eventually running away back to the reservation. Nannie realizes that Whiteshield's behavior is caused by his suffering, his longing to fulfill his identity as a warrior. Nannie's assimilation may lull the reader into forgetting the painful history of the school. Nannie's best friend, Pretty Eagle, is the only Native character who successfully resists assimilation. She comforts the other students by reminding them of their identity and traditions. She, however, is buried alive when she falls into a trance, presenting a grisly symbol for the way this system of schooling buries the true identity of its Native students.

Although Rinaldi has received praise for her research and historical accuracy in previous novels, in her treatment of this sensitive topic she has received criticism. As indicated earlier, much of this criticism initially appeared on Web discussion sites and was then finalized in reviews in Oyate and *Multicultural Review*. The reviewers are Marlene Atleo, Naomi Caldwell, Barbara Landis, Jean Mendoza, Deborah Miranda, Debbie Reese, LaVera Rose,

Beverly Slapin, and Cynthia Smith. They criticize Rinaldi's depiction of Nannie Little Rose's experience at Carlisle on several fronts: lack of literary quality, lack of cultural authenticity, and lack of historical correctness. The reviewers say the novel lacks "consistency and logic" (*Oyate*, 7). They do not think that it is plausible that a child like Nannie would have been given a diary by her teachers at Carlisle, nor would she have written any negative comments about her white teachers whom she feared. Nannie's concerns are not authentic: she "romantically obsesses over the concepts 'bravery,' 'honor,' and 'nobleness'" (*Oyate*, 14). In general, the reviewers conclude that Rinaldi gets into problems of stereotyping and perspective in this story.

The reviewers also cite over a dozen factual errors in the novel. For example, Nannie mentions Chief Sitting Bull of the Cheyenne Nation (*Heart*, 14). The reviewers say his real name is Tatanka Iotanka, a Hunkpapa Lakota, and he was a spiritual leader, not a chief. In another place Rinaldi depicts Spotted Tail's visit to Carlisle in 1880 and his decision to take his children back to Rosebud (*Heart*, 121). The Oyate reviewers say that this depiction is not true. They cite George Hyde's *Spotted Tail's Folk: A History of the Brule Sioux* (1979) as a true description of this event. The children tried to escape and hide themselves so they could leave with Spotted Tail (*Oyate*, 9). They disagree with Rinaldi's conclusion that graduates were able to make a living away from the reservation (*Heart*, 182) because most of the graduates actually ended up working in Indian service on a reservation or in one of the off-reservation schools, modeled on Carlisle (*Oyate*, 9).

The Oyate reviewers also criticize the cultural authenticity of Rinaldi's story. They do not believe Nannie Little Rose would have seen herself or her brother or her people in the way Rinaldi depicts. They do not think Nannie "would have been misinformed about her own people" as several of her comments suggest (*Oyate*, 10). Nannie would not have criticized her brother Whiteshield because "Brothers and sisters have a special bond in Lakota society that was even more pronounced in this time period. They were taught to honor each other above all others, including spouses" (*Oyate*, 11). Further, Nannie's father would not have asked her to take on a vision quest (*Heart*, 30) because "that would have been her brother's responsibility" (*Oyate*, 12). Overall, the Oyate reviewers conclude that Rinaldi has relied on stereotyped images of Native Americans. They believe that despite her research, her lack of experience in this community has led her to make errors. She, like other authors writing from outside the culture, may "unknowingly mimic misconceptions or stereotypes inherent in the research material, and still others may 'whitewash' history to make the non-Native audience more comfortable with issues like stolen land and forced assimilation" (*Oyate*, 17).

Debbie Reese says, "In writing this story, Rinaldi has done a tremendous disservice to the memories of the dead children whose names she used, to their families, to Native children today, and to any child who reads and believes what Rinaldi has written" (April 12, 1999, NCSS discussion board).

Scholastic, the publisher of the Dear America series, responded to these criticisms. They believe Rinaldi wrote with the intention of "unearthing the horrors of Carlisle" (April 23, 1999, Child_Lit). Rinaldi says in "About the Author" that she wanted to tell the "heart-wrenching accounts of young Native Americans shipped across the country, away from their tribal culture, families, and familiar surroundings, to live in a hostile and strange environment" (*Heart*, 195). Scholastic also defended their process of ensuring historical accuracy. During the writing of the novel, they contacted Barbara Landis at the Cumberland County Historical Society, who recommended Genevieve Bell, Ph.D., to check the accuracy of the manuscript. Since Debbie Reese also contacted Barbara Landis, Scholastic concludes that they both used the same source to ensure accuracy. Scholastic says that of the factual errors pointed out in the Oyate review, only one was addressed by Dr. Bell. Other issues, pointed out by Bell, were reviewed by the author and many changes were made. "In some cases where changes were not made it was because the author had documented research that conflicted. And many of the broader issues—like the appropriation of names . . . became a matter of judgment and point of view" (April 23, 1999, Child_Lit).

Scholastic did decide to make one change in the series. Even before *My Heart Is on the Ground* was published, critics had been negative about the epilogue that appears at the end of each novel in the Dear America series. It describes what happens to the main characters after the events covered in the diary.[20] Some critics said the epilogues were misleading, causing confusion about the fictional nature of the diaries. Scholastic plans to give a clearer, more prominent disclaimer in the series, reminding readers that the books are fiction.

BRINGING HISTORY TO LIFE

Despite such controversy, Rinaldi remains committed to her underlying purpose. She writes for two reasons: to help teens see that there isn't that much difference between themselves and people in the past, and to create a new sense of pride in them as citizens of the United States. In the note to *The Fifth of March* Rinaldi makes a connection between the Los Angeles riots in 1992 and the Boston Massacre. She says, "It is by drawing such lines between the past and the present that I hope to help young readers realize that some historic events happened because of the everyday feelings of the people involved, whose concerns and aspirations were not so very different from those of young readers today" (*March*, 323).

Rinaldi also believes history can be a powerful source of pride for young people. She says, "We've had enough of putting down the country . . . children have no pride, they have no respect, they have no feeling of self worth." Rinaldi writes to counter these negative forces by emphasizing "the fact of what we have become and how we became it." She wants to get beyond the myths, to the essential human stories that make history.

• 2 •

From Journalist to Fiction Writer

$\mathcal{I}$n the twenty years since she began writing novels for young adults, Ann Rinaldi has published, on the average, a novel every year. She has written twenty-one historical fiction novels since 1986. However, her first novels were realistic, focusing on the contemporary identity problems of her main characters, adolescent girls. It wasn't until she was writing her fourth novel of this kind that Rinaldi discovered her real subject in historical fiction. Today, her contemporary novels are out of print, but they show how she developed her themes as she wrote about young adult experiences. In these novels she concentrated on several subjects—father–daughter and sibling relationships and the coming of age of adolescent characters—subjects she would also explore in her historical fiction. Certain themes emerged that continue to be important in all her fiction, such as learning the difference between appearance and reality, making difficult moral choices, and forging identity. These novels are based on Rinaldi's own experiences growing up, raising children, working as a columnist for the newspapers, and learning about herself as a writer.

WARTIME CHILDHOOD

Ann Rinaldi always wanted to write from the time she was a child. She loved memorizing and reciting poems in school and started writing poetry in her own "little book" when she was about ten years old. Like many girls growing up in the 1930s and 1940s, Rinaldi read all the Louisa May Alcott books, the Lassie books, and *My Friend Flicka*. For a long time she felt these books, which spoke to her in a personal way, were written just for her. Losing herself in books and discovering herself through her writing were an important part of her growing up. Rinaldi says, "I always wanted to be a writer, but I didn't know how I was going to get there."

Rinaldi had a difficult childhood. Her mother died about a month after she was born and her father remarried within a year. For a short time as a baby, Rinaldi lived with her Aunt Margaret and Uncle Dan in Brooklyn. Rinaldi remembers them as wonderful people with a household that was a magnet for the extended family. It was the Depression and whenever anyone needed help—the maiden aunt, the bachelor uncle, the husband's brother who got sick—they came to Margaret's. Rinaldi says, "That's the way it was then." Also Margaret had three teenagers of her own, so there was always lots going on, people coming and going, and Ann was the center of attention. Rinaldi has vivid memories of this time. She remembers sitting on her uncle's lap, watching him swing a gold pocket watch back and forth to amuse her. She recalls cousins, holding her by the arms and swinging her over cracks in the sidewalk, and her aunt calling across a crowded room, "Watch the baby, watch the baby." Rinaldi credits their care and loving attention as laying the foundation for all the loving relationships in the rest of her life. Rinaldi says when she was about three years old, her father came to take her home to New Jersey to live with her stepmother and four older siblings, and "the only happy part of my childhood ended" (*SATA*, vol. 51, 150).

Rinaldi didn't know much about her mother when she was growing up. In the note to *Wolf by the Ears*, Rinaldi says, "I never knew her family or even saw a picture of her until I was married."[1] Her stepmother didn't want the children to talk about their mother. Rinaldi says, "She wanted it to be known that she was our mother, but I knew different." In later years, Rinaldi learned that her mother was well educated and talented in sculpture. She was sweet and gentle and devoted to her children and home.

In addition to Rinaldi's personal loss, her childhood took place in "a serious world, a world where we were losing the war for the first year or so and everything was harsh." War dominated her consciousness; she was seven when the war started and eleven when it ended. She remembers rationing, air raids at school, radio programs about killing the enemy. In the note to *Keep Smiling Through*, Rinaldi says, "We children on the home front were expected to integrate all the horrific images of war into our lives and not only adjust, but do our chores and schoolwork, save our pennies and buy war stamps, and give up such things as sugar, extra shoes, and all hope of new toys—and keep our mouths shut and stay in the background, too, while the grown-ups around us went about the grim business of survival in a world gone mad."[2]

In her teen years, Rinaldi recalls feeling isolated. She was not allowed to participate in extracurricular activities, and so she found herself mostly "on the outside," observing others. Looking back, Rinaldi thinks that at the time there were two ways for her to understand her life: either there was something wrong with her and she didn't deserve anything, or there was something wrong with her situation. She thinks she was "almost trained to be a writer by everything that happened" in her childhood because she was constantly trying to figure things out. She got no support from her father or stepmother.

Rinaldi's father was a newspaper manager involved in the business end of journalism. She says, he "did everything he could to prevent me from becoming a writer" (*SATA*, vol. 51, 150). He discouraged her from setting career goals and didn't believe in college for girls. Her parents wanted her to work, so Rinaldi was channeled into business classes. After graduation from high school, she became a secretary, moving through several different jobs.

In 1960, when she was twenty-six, Ann married Ronald Rinaldi, and soon they had two children. This is when Rinaldi returned to her writing because she had the time. When the children were babies, she actually completed four novels for adults, sending them off to publishers and collecting rejection slips. She can't even remember the stories of these novels today, but thinks they were "terrible."

THE NEWSPAPER SCHOOL OF WRITING

Rinaldi's school of writing was the newspapers. In 1968 she asked Wally Conover, editor of her local newspaper, the weekly *Somerset Messenger Gazette*, to let her do a column. This was the opportunity Rinaldi wanted—to write and see her writing in print. Within the year, Rinaldi had syndicated her column to eighteen daily and weekly newspapers in the tri-state area, and she was ready to take on another challenge. In 1970 she called F. Gilman Spencer, editor of *The Trentonian*, a daily, about writing a column for that newspaper. She took samples of her writing to her first meeting with Spencer, and he hired her in five minutes to write two columns a week. She recalls that he was impressed with her writing and asked her in amazement, "Where did you come from?"

During these years her children were young, and she worked at home. At first she was writing for the women's section of the paper, drawing on her experiences raising two young children as well as local news. She says, "I raised my children in the column"; everyone knew about the Rinaldi children. She also wrote about other kinds of human interest. Many of the social agencies in Trenton—soup kitchens, the battered women's shelter, the Salvation Army—would come to her regularly to tell the stories of the people who needed aid. Rinaldi interviewed all kinds of people: prisoners, political personalities, patients on a burn ward, people in the news, and common folks.

First, working part time for *The Trentonian*, Rinaldi was writing feature stories and even editorials. Her column was on the front page. In 1975 Spencer won the Pulitzer prize and was leaving the newspaper; before he left he hired Rinaldi full time. In her newspaper writing, Rinaldi was noted for the quality of her stories, the human interest element. Whenever a news event would occur, Rinaldi would talk to people on the street. She was interested in getting the people's story, the people's reaction to events. Rinaldi recalls the 1970s as interesting times. "We had the women's movement, the civil rights movement, the Vietnam War." *The Trentonian* was full of talented people and writers were given total freedom. Rinaldi says, "I was all over the place, covering everything; it was very exciting."

These are the years when Rinaldi learned to write. She learned how to conduct an interview, how to take notes, how to edit her own writing, how to produce on deadline. Most important, she "learned how to know a story." She was a columnist with the paper for twenty-one years, until 1991.

FIRST FICTION WRITING

In 1979 Rinaldi was a successful columnist; she had received the New Jersey Press Association first-place award for a newspaper column; she was in love with the newspaper business and devoted to her profession. She was also an unpublished fiction writer. She decided to see if she was still interested in writing fiction, if she had other stories inside her. From her earlier writing for adults, she had kept a 10,000-word short story, which had a fourteen-year-old protagonist. She showed this manuscript to a friend, Barbara Cohen, a successful children's writer (known for *Thank You, Jackie Robinson* and *Molly's Pilgrim*). After reading the manuscript, Cohen told Rinaldi that she had the centerpiece of a young adult novel. She encouraged Rinaldi to expand the story and promised to show it to her literary agent. This was the encouragement Rinaldi needed. She wrote the novel, *Term Paper*, quickly, and sold it to the first publisher who read it.

In the opening of *Term Paper* (1980), the main character, Nicki, says, "I've got to write this. There isn't any getting out of it. My brother Tony has me between a rock and a hard place. And the space in between is getting narrower all the time."[3] Nicki could almost be speaking for Rinaldi who, describing the creation of this first novel eighteen years later, recalls that the writing was almost unstoppable. "It was such a pure, creative impulse." Wanting to get the story down as quickly as possible, Rinaldi says that she didn't even stop to break it into chapters. Writing this first novel was an exhilarating and liberating experience for her. She believes, "You never regain that first creative impulse." After the first novel, writers, necessarily, have to think about the market they're writing for or the age of their readers. This doesn't have to box the writer in, but it's not quite the same as writing the first novel.

In *Term Paper* Rinaldi explored subjects that were close to her own experiences. Rinaldi believes that writers, like everyone else, "come with baggage," but writers are different because they explore the baggage. She says, "When you're a writer, you've got to get rid of that baggage first before you can do anything else." Rinaldi says, even today, that she had to tell the story of her childhood in her novels; she had to deal with her father, "who had haunted me all my life." Rinaldi remembers her father blaming her for the death of her mother. She says, "The blame that is put on you as a child never leaves you. The guilt never leaves." Rinaldi also recalls growing up with the fear of losing her father. He threatened the children that he would have a heart attack if they didn't behave. In a biographical statement written when *Term Paper* was published, Rinaldi says, "I wrote my novel because the characters had been part of me for years. Most of the motivation came from my own life. Family relationships, especially the tremendous influence older siblings have over younger ones, have always intrigued me."[4] Rinaldi also thinks some of her themes arise from her sense of alienation, of not knowing her mother, of losing the family she knew as a baby. Like her favorite Southern writers, Rinaldi writes, at least on one level, to deal with her sense of loss.

TERM PAPER: WRITING CAN HEAL

In *Term Paper*, Nicki is trying to understand herself in relation to her father and brothers. She blames herself for her father's death. She fears losing her brother Larry to drugs, and she has a rocky relationship with her older brother and guardian, Tony, who thinks she's out of control. Six months after her father's death, Tony, who has become her substitute English teacher, assigns her to write a "term paper," hoping it will force Nicki to deal with her guilt and unresolved feelings. He wants her to dump the "baggage" she's carrying around inside, so she can heal.

The term paper turns into an extended memoir of Nicki's short life, showing the sources of her insecurity. The facts are laid out quickly: Nicki's mother died when she was born; her father decided he was too busy to make time for her; and Carol, her brother Tony's wife, acts as a "sort of a mother" until Tony returns from the Vietnam War. Then Tony takes over raising Nicki, but he keeps up the charade that her father is really in control. One night Nicki finally confronts her father about his selfish behavior, and he suffers a massive heart attack. Nicki feels a deep sense of guilt on top of her already deep sense of insecurity and confusion. But writing the term paper helps. Nicki begins to understand her feelings, which helps her work out a relationship with Tony.

SIBLING RELATIONSHIPS IN *PROMISES ARE FOR KEEPING*

Term Paper was accepted by the first publisher who read it and soon was published in paperback as well. Rinaldi didn't start out thinking of herself as a young adult writer, but after this first novel was so successful, she began work on a sequel, and *Promises Are for Keeping* (1982) followed within a year. Rinaldi recalls, "I was addicted to newspapers—that was my profession." But with the publication of her first novel, she suddenly found herself with two full-time careers, plus being a wife and raising two high school age children. Now her life was all about time. She recalls always thinking, "I've got the next day's column to write. I have dinner to do tonight. I have another book I want to write. I need the time. Where am I going to get the time?" As a newspaper columnist Rinaldi had learned to write any place, any time—outside, on buses, at election headquarters on election night when half of the people are drunk and rowdy. She had also learned to make deadlines. This training was invaluable. After a full day's work, Rinaldi would write at night after supper, using the dining room table as her desk. She made the time to write her next novel.

In *Promises Are for Keeping*, Rinaldi decided to follow Nicki as she goes into her sophomore year in high school. A year after her father's death, Nicki still feels quite a bit of guilt. Describing herself early in the novel, Nicki says, "I caused my father's death . . . because I argued with him when his heart was bad."[5] She also continues to carry around a deep insecurity.

Nicki doesn't have a very high opinion of herself. She says, "I have this knack for messing up relationships. I mess up every relationship I have, sooner or later" (*Promises*, 14). However, at this point Nicki has arrived at a kind of truce with Tony, her older brother. She describes their relationship: "It's like coming home every time Tony hugs me like that. And we have years behind us, years of arguments and tears, of pullings-apart and comings-together. Years of moments when his stern demands made me hate him, nothing less. . . . But always he'd allow me to talk back. Always he'd listen and be fair" (*Promises*, 46). Larry, Nicki's other brother, is not as understanding. In this novel, Larry, who is a physician, has just been named co-guardian with Tony. Overeacting to new responsibility, Larry tries to control Nicki's every move.

This is a difficult time for Nicki. Not only does she continue to have unresolved feelings to deal with, she is also vulnerable to peer pressure, which gets her into more trouble than she can handle. First one of her friends puts in a prank call to the governor's office, which brings the state police to Larry's office. Then Nicki tries to steal birth control pills for her best friend.

Larry decides something has to be done to teach Nicki responsibility, so he signs her up for the hospital volunteer program—the candystripers. Nicki hates Larry for doing this to her. Not only does she hate hospitals, but this work forces her to give up her job as school newspaper photographer and miss out on high school football games. She says, "My wrath *was* inside me like a wrecking ball. I could feel it slamming against my rib cage. . . . And it alienated me from any decent feeling I'd ever had" (*Promises*, 104). Nicki decides to give Larry "the silent treatment." She can't understand how Larry, who has always been the "softer" brother, the one she could turn to, has changed so drastically. Nicki loves and hates Larry at the same time but can't deal with her feelings. "I can't cope with how I feel. And I don't even want to try" (*Promises*, 105).

At the hospital, Nicki meets people who give her a different view of her brother. She hears about his care and compassion and the sacrifices he makes to help people. Tony gives her an image of Larry's vulnerability when he describes how Larry held their mother on the night she died. Nicki begins to think less about her anger and more about her brother's feelings. Seeing Nicki's reaction to his punishment, Larry also realizes that he has to be more sensitive to Nicki and not impose his will.

Both Nicki and Larry have a reconciliation that actually saves Larry's life. Because of her change in attitude, Nicki is more sensitive to Larry and detects that he needs help one night. He tells her to stay away from him, but Nicki knows this isn't like him. She discovers thieves, part of a drug ring, holding Larry at gunpoint and stealing drugs from his medical office. In the end, the bond between Larry and Nicki, their "promise," or what Tony calls "karma," is more important than who is in control. Both Nicki and Larry have to learn to give and take and build the trust that lets their relationship grow.

NEW PROTAGONIST FOR *BUT IN THE FALL I'M LEAVING*

In 1985 Rinaldi made a switch to a new publisher, Holiday House, and created a new adolescent character, Brieanna (Brie for short) McQuade, daughter of a small-town newspaper owner and editor. Brie's father is a composite, Rinaldi says, of the many fine editors she encountered in her newspaper work. Descriptions of the professional responsibilities and the day-to-day job of a journalist, drawn from Rinaldi's career, create background for this and the next novel. For example, Brie describes how her father approves the "black line"(headline) and lead stories every night. He takes seriously his responsibility as a journalist to investigate issues in the community. In this novel, he works with the police on an undercover sting operation against prostitution.

Brie is a more mature version of Nicki, but with similar identity problems. She doesn't cry all the time and she isn't quite so hard on herself, but she is carrying around lots of ambivalent feelings about her mother. Brie resents that her mother doesn't make time for her, but she also thinks things would be different, better, if she lived with her mother. She respects her father, but she's not sure that this feeling is the same as love. She's confused and depressed by her situation.

There is another problem. Brie senses hidden undercurrents and even an inexplicable spiritual connection to Miss Emily, one of Waltham's leading citizens. She notices the "strange relationship" between her father and Emily and thinks that understanding this relationship would help her understand her father better and maybe herself. Brie doesn't know that Miss Emily is her maternal grandmother. Brie's mother left when she was just two, and her father feared that Miss Emily would turn Brie against him. He decided to conceal her identity, and then it became too late to tell Brie the truth.

At the opening of the novel, Brie vandalizes Miss Emily's house as a teenage prank and is sentenced to do community service working for her. Like the term paper that Nicki is forced to write, this probation helps Brie learn about Miss Emily and, eventually, herself. As she works with Miss Emily, Brie begins to respect and admire the ways in which Emily works to improve community life.

When Miss Emily dies, Brie's mother reveals her grandmother's true identity. Brie feels betrayed and manipulated and blames her father for the deception. She has lost her grandmother without getting to know her while everyone else knew the truth. Her older brother, Kevin, helps Brie sort out her feelings. She begins to understand the complexity of why people act as they do as she thinks about the motives of her father and mother. In time she accepts her father's mistake, as one based on love, while she realizes her mother's selfishness. Brie faces difficult truths about both of the people she loves the most.

BRIE GROWS UP IN *THE GOOD SIDE OF MY HEART*

Rinaldi's fourth realistic novel (1987) picks up Brie's story a year after her grandmother's death. Brie, at sixteen, has adjusted to life without illusions about her mother. She says, for now anyway, my mother isn't "part of my life anymore."[6] Brie's emotional life revolves around pleasing her father, sustaining her close relationship with her priest-brother, Kevin, and meeting her first "serious" boyfriend, her best friend's brother, Josh Falcon.

Brie gets involved with Josh, a senior who enrolls in Waltham High after being kicked out of a military academy, despite her best friend's warnings and her father's concern that Josh is too old for her. Brie has heard the rumors that his dismissal "had something to do with a girl," and she senses that he is hiding something about himself. Complications develop almost immediately when Brie and Josh go on a high school overnight trip, and Brie lies and hides drugs for one of the seniors in a mistaken attempt to protect Josh. Also when Josh doesn't respond to her as she expects him to, Brie begins to wonder about her attractiveness. When Josh doesn't seem interested in kissing her, Brie pushes him until he reveals that he is a homosexual.

In the rest of the novel, Brie has to deal with this revelation and the complications caused by her actions. And this time, her usual confidant, Kevin, has too many problems of his own to help. Brie realizes, even before Kevin, that he has become involved with an attractive social worker at his parish. She fears that he is thinking about leaving the priesthood and knows how this decision would devastate his life.

Brie has to learn to forget about herself and concentrate on what others are going through. Her father helps her sort out her feelings by showing her how to accept Josh and help Kevin deal with his crisis of self-doubt. As in Rinaldi's other realistic novels, an adolescent girls faces problems in her relationships with others and gains maturity in the process.

RELATIONSHIP WITH BROTHERS

These brief descriptions of Rinaldi's four realistic novels show that sibling relationships are an important subject for her. In each novel, she creates younger sister and older brother characters and spins the plot around their changing relationship. In the first novels, the sibling relationships play out as a battle for control, with older brothers assuming their dominance. But in the later novels, the brother–sister relationship changes and grows in depth as the two people recognize each other as equal individuals who can offer each other support and advice. So Rinaldi's conception of the brother–sister relationship encompasses a wide range of behaviors from authoritarian to egalitarian. In Rinaldi's overall portrayal of sibling relationships, she shows how more equal and mutually supporting behaviors among siblings lead to more positive relationships.

In *Term Paper*, Tony, who is about fifteen years older than Nicki, sees it as his duty to discipline a "spoiled rotten" kid. His heavy-handed approach, however, causes Nicki to feel unloved and resentful. When she is writing the required term paper, Nicki recalls one of her early battles with Tony. One night she refused to eat her dinner and Tony spanked her. Nicki, outraged and hurt, cried violently, until suddenly she heard a noise. Tony was crying too. Scared, Nicki promised never to be "bad" again. Now she resents his emotional hold over her. Nicki doesn't realize that Tony was crying because he also was scared. He had let his anger and frustration get out of control.

Tony tries to protect Nicki from making wrong choices by socializing her to the submissive behaviors often expected of young women in American society. Nicki is supposed to do what her brother says, without asking questions; when she acts more independently, he calls her difficult or disrespectful. Tony unerringly uses Nicki's deepest insecurities to control her. If she doesn't do what he says, he threatens to send her away and have nothing more to do with her. This is a powerful threat to Nicki, who already feels insecure about where she belongs. She doesn't have the stability of a permanent home and parents. Instead she lives between two houses, her father's and the apartment of her brother, spending some nights at one house and some at the other.

Tony often chooses control over love. Even though he is the adult, he refuses to back down over one argument and won't see Nicki for almost a week to punish her. Also when Nicki reveals her guilt about her father's death and her fears of abandonment in the term paper, Tony gives her the silent treatment for three weeks. Nicki says, "I went from disappointment to depression" (*Term*, 194). Tony tries to excuse his behavior, but in reality he needs time to deal with the truth of what his sister has written. He can't blame Nicki for her father's death. He knew the gravity of his father's illness, but he didn't tell her. Instead he used the situation as a test of Nicki's obedience. Tony realizes that, like the time when he spanked Nicki, he put his need for control over the emotional needs of his sister. In the end Tony achieves a reconciliation with her. He takes some of the blame and begins to recognize the complexities of his sister's feelings. He realizes Nicki is an independent person who has a right to the truth about her father, so she can deal with her feelings. He tries to meet her halfway.

TIES THAT BIND

In *Promises Are for Keeping*, Rinaldi looks at Nicki's relationship with her other brother, Larry, the brother who was always there for her. Nicki remembers, "All my life he'd been the tender, loving brother, the gentle one, always willing to listen and advise" (*Promises*, 90). But Larry changes when he is made her co-guardian with Tony. Fearful about his new responsibility, Larry wants to treat Nicki as a domineering and judgmental parent would. According to Larry, Nicki is "running too wild." He's afraid of how she handles herself with boys; he wants her to do better in school; he's mad because she isn't going to church; and, in general, he thinks she's "spoiled rotten." When Nicki makes mistakes, Larry takes it personally. He accuses her, "But we tried with you, didn't we? Haven't we been the best of brothers? . . . Then *why*! How could you do this to us?" (*Promises*, 88).

Part of Larry's reaction to Nicki's behavior has to do with his own compulsion to control everything in his life. Larry has turned inward his own resentments toward their father when he was growing up. While he hated his father's control, Larry still looked for the "approval" his father withheld; when it wasn't forthcoming, he reacted by becoming a perfectionist. Now when Larry can't control things, he gets depressed, angry, and makes "everybody miserable" (*Promises*, 162).

Tony knows Larry has to work out his "parenting" in his own way. He knows Larry will have to change in order to have a relationship with Nicki, but he also believes that their essential bond as brother and sister will help the relationship survive. Tony tells Nicki, "Don't mess with the bonds that tie us together. . . . They're deep and mysterious and have dark undersides that shouldn't be messed with. Work it out somehow inside yourself" (*Promises*, 104). Tony is talking to Nicki, but also to himself and Larry. These are the ties that bind: being brother and sister, realizing they all share the loss of their mother, trying to deal with their feelings toward their father, knowing everyone makes mistakes.

Larry has to learn to respect their "bonds" just as much as Nicki. Larry signs up Nicki as a volunteer at the hospital without being sensitive to her needs. Later, he tells Nicki, "I had no idea you'd take it all so badly. I wouldn't have done what I did if I'd had any idea how it would affect you" (*Promises*, 128). Larry discovers that his love for Nicki is more important than his control. He doesn't want to repeat what his father did. He lets Nicki know that he will always be there for her and gives her the distance to deal with her feelings. He tells her, "I don't believe that people have to smother each other just because they're related. I went through that with the old man. I won't do that to you" (*Promises*, 129). Instead their relationship becomes, as Tony says, "like . . . a promise you have to keep to each other all your lives" (*Promises*, 150). Larry learns that being a parent means more than making rules, and that there is no set way he has to act toward Nicki. In the end he says, "A person doesn't ask the right questions of himself until he becomes a parent" (Promises, 186). The challenge for Larry is to ask questions, not try to give Nicki all the answers.

MORE EQUAL RELATIONSHIPS IN *BUT IN THE FALL I'M LEAVING* AND *THE GOOD SIDE OF MY HEART*

In the next two novels, the older brother is not trying to fill the role of the father, and the relationship between siblings moves toward even greater mutual support. In *But in the Fall I'm Leaving*, Kevin is an important confidant to his sister, but from a somewhat paternalistic position. Kevin is a priest in the Catholic Church and is usually called on when Brie is having problems. But he is also a loved older brother. Despite their age difference of fifteen years, Kevin has always been close to Brie. He took care of her when she was younger and was always involved in her growing up. He knows how hard it is for Brie to grow up without a mother, with a priest for a brother, and how defensive she feels.

Brie finds herself confiding in Kevin, even when she doesn't want to, because she trusts that as a priest he won't violate her confidence. With him she has "all the secrecy of the confessional."[7] Also, Kevin has gone through the same experience of losing their mother. In one part of her mind, Brie suspects that Kevin works with the poor in the Newark slums in reaction to the materialistic values their mother chose when she left the family. Brie says, "I suspected Mom's leaving has a lot to do with some spring snapping inside him. Mom left for a career and the good life. And I had it figured that Kev went completely the opposite way, rejecting everything of material value" (*Fall*, 35). She also knows that he hasn't forgiven his mother; like her, he has his own "black hole" to deal with.

Kevin doesn't want to be just a priest to Brie; he wants to be her brother, too. He says, "I need you as a sister. I need somebody I can be friends with. There aren't many people I can get close to" (*Fall*, 79). Unlike the brothers in Rinaldi's first novels, Kevin has already decided that he doesn't want to be Brie's father figure, controlling her behavior. He wants to help her and have her help him. When Brie is angry at her father, Kevin doesn't tell her what to do. But he insists that she face the truth about their mother. Then he gives her the space to sort it all out. Brie says, "The most important thing he ever did for me was to leave me alone on that island that day" (*Fall*, 249).

The Good Side of My Heart shows how the relationship between Brie and Kevin achieves a deeper mutuality. Kevin is still Brie's confidant. She says, "He's chased off my demons, listened to me, seen the blackness in my soul, and loved me anyway" (*Good Side*, 70). Kevin asks hard questions, detects misrepresentations for the lies they really are, and insists on difficult choices. Kevin wants Brie to take responsibility for her actions. He tells her, "We have that choice. To become bitter and resentful or to see things out of the good side of our hearts" (*Good Side*, 248). But their relationship is not one-sided. Kevin confides in Brie also. He gives her "the same degree of honesty" that she has given to him. He confesses that he has broken his vow of chastity and doubts his ability to help others as a priest. He reaches out to Brie for help. Brie is scared and wonders, "Did he expect me to help him? Me? I supposed that he did. He was still my brother. But what could I possibly say to make it all right?" (*Good Side*, 256). When Brie argues with him and gets him to examine himself, Kevin listens and takes courage and hope. Brie has helped him. He says, "I make the mistake, constantly, of still thinking of you as a little girl. I can't do that anymore" (*Good Side*, 260).

So Rinaldi portrays a full range of brotherly behaviors, from paternalistic and one-sided to fraternal and equal. She shows how the sibling relationship can lead to growth and mutual benefit for both persons. Both the adult and the adolescent, the older brother and the sister, can give and take emotional support from one another.

FATHER-DAUGHTER RELATIONSHIPS

Just as Rinaldi's depictions of brother-sister relationships shift from authoritarian to more equal and multidimensional, so too her portrayal of fathers in these novels shifts dramatically. The father in *Term Paper* is distant and self-centered, but by the last novel, Brie's father is almost idealized as a loving, caring person.

In *Term Paper*, Nicki's father is a restless, careless man who tramples on others' feelings. He deserts the family, and then returns and pretends nothing has happened. He also manipulates people. When Aunt Rosemary, her mother's sister, tells Nicki about her father's past extramarital affairs, he forces Rosemary to leave town. He pays off Larry's girlfriend to get rid of her because she doesn't fit his image of the kind of woman Larry should be dating. He can't be bothered to raise Nicki and turns over his responsibility to her older brother, but still wants her love and respect. About the time Nicki is in the seventh grade, he has a heart attack and then uses his health as a barrier against her needs. Nicki learns to read his moods, whether "remote fondness" or total aloofness, and not react.

When Nicki confronts her father, he justifies himself, saying all the children have survived, come out even stronger because of their experiences. But Nicki won't give this to him. She knows that Larry isn't better off—he's on drugs—and Tony has had to fight hard for years to recover from his father's desertion. Nicki wants her father to realize that the kids "got screwed up," that they have been terribly hurt. These are the last words she says to her father as he collapses and dies. Although Nicki is full of guilt, she also knows that there is a reason for her unloving feelings. She asks, "Are you supposed to love somebody just because he's your father?" (*Term*, 44). She recognizes that there is more to fathering than giving birth. It's the nurturing and love that her father fails to give her that she desperately misses.

MORE POSITIVE FATHER FIGURES

Having put aside some personal "baggage" with her portrayal of the selfish father in *Term Paper*, Rinaldi was ready to create a positive father figure in Jim McQuade in her third realistic novel, *But in the Fall I'm Leaving*. McQuade is a single parent, deeply involved in both his job as a newspaper editor and also his responsibility for raising Brie. He thinks he hasn't always done a good job with her, but at least he's tried. He tells her, "Your mom's leaving and the fact that I've been too immersed in my career prevented me from giving you the quality of fatherhood you should have had. But I've been here for you, and I intend to keep on being here for you. That's not much, but you'll always know what to expect and what not to expect. You can count on me, Brie, always" (*Fall*, 30). Brie knows that her father is good at figuring things out and can get to the bottom of her problems. But at times she doesn't want his logic; she isn't ready to face his explanations. Jim McQuade is smart enough to know that Brie needs to figure things out on her own. He wants to help Brie grow up, but he knows how important it is for her to face the truth in her own way.

In *The Good Side of My Heart* Brie's father is an even more positive role model. Jim McQuade loves being a dad. He has high expectations for Brie, and when he gets angry, it isn't arbitrary but part of his larger worldview. Brie recognizes his character: "He's a decent, gentle man who has a long fuse, but you don't ever want to light it. . . . It's all part of his built-in sense of outrage and passion for justice" (*Good Side*, 30 and 105).

McQuade knows that he has to stand back and let his children have a chance to make their own choices. He doesn't tell Brie what to do; he waits to be asked. Brie realizes, "He was a parent all right, and he let you know it when you did something wrong, but lately, it seemed that he was waiting to be asked for advice instead of giving it so readily" (*Good Side*, 264). His attitude gives his children a sense of security and possibility as they sort out life for themselves.

GIRLS COMING OF AGE

In depicting family relationships, Rinaldi always focuses on the changes going on in the adolescent girls. In these four novels, Nicki and Brie grow up as they face their insecurities and develop more realistic ideas about themselves and others. They move from isolation to integration into the community. In other words, they go through a process of maturing or coming of age.

In *Term Paper*, Nicki can't talk to her brothers about what happened on the night their father died. She blocks their questions, refusing to face her guilt, because she fears they won't love her anymore. But writing the term paper, Nicki begins to understand her painful alienation. She recognizes why she blames her father and feels betrayed when she learns that he had a mistress even when her mother was alive. Looking back on her hysterical reaction, Nicki realizes, "I was hitting everything in my life I couldn't cope with, everything I couldn't fix. I was hitting out at my father for never being a father. . . . I was hitting out at myself for saying the words that had broken my father's heart the moment before he died" (*Term*, 176).

Nicki learns not to hate her father by watching her brothers, knowing that they had resentments and yet they "did everything right" (*Term*, 199).

Larry tells her, "There are no absolutes in life . . . we're all a mixture of good and bad . . . everybody, including the old man" (*Term*, 184). Realizing the truth of what he says from her own experiences, Nicki knows she can learn to forgive her father and even herself. She takes the first steps toward self-acceptance.

Brie in *But in the Fall I'm Leaving* doesn't have Nicki's guilt. After all, her mother left when she was just two years old, so she doesn't blame herself. But Brie tries to hold on to a fantasy version of her mother because she wants "a shot at having a mother for a change." She thinks, "Maybe I just want to see what she's like. Find out for myself by living with her" (*Fall*, 157–158). She doesn't want to accept her father's assessment that her mother is only willing to give her "gifts and money and promises," not commitment. Brie doesn't want to accept other people's version of the truth.

But Brie soon learns how difficult it is to know the truth. She has to decide about her mother's motives for revealing her grandmother's identity. In the balance hangs her whole picture of her mother and what life could be like with her. It would be easy to blame her father and refuse to have anything to do with him. But Kevin doesn't let her take the easy way out; she can't just act like a hurt child. She says, "If only he would demand or scold. . . . Then I could argue and be snotty" (*Fall*, 225). Instead Kevin asks Brie to face "her demons." He treats her like an adult and asks her to think carefully and make her judgments wisely. He also thinks she is ready for the whole truth. He tells her, "Mom knew Dad hadn't told you about Miss Emily being your grandmother. She knew you didn't know" (*Fall*, 233–234). Although it is painful, Brie has to face her mother's motives: her mother wanted to discredit Brie's father, no matter how much Brie got hurt.

Brie grows up when she faces reality. She sees her mother and father for what they are—flawed people who make bad, even selfish, decisions. She reconciles with her father at the end but is unable to deal with her feelings toward her mother. She sees that her father acted out of love even though he made mistakes. On the other hand, her mother used her to get back at her father. Brie wonders, "How could Mom *do* such a thing to me?" (*Fall*, 245) She feels cheated that she would never know her grandmother, but she also realizes that she doesn't really know her mother. She says, "I buried both of them on my island that day. Miss Emily and my mother. It would be a long time before I could resolve what each of them had done to me" (*Fall*, 247).

In *The Good Side of My Heart* Brie continues her process of coming of age. Brie has begun to sort out appearance from reality and to see the ambiguities in human behavior, but she is still dependent. She describes herself as a little kid "on the top step of a ladder" (*Good Side*, 73). She links this feeling of dependency to a traumatic event when she was five. To teach her not to grab ornaments off the Christmas tree, Kevin set her on the top step of a ladder and left the room. Brie remembers feeling helpless and frightened, until her brother took her down. As a teen, she still feels like this. She is controlled by her father's and brother's values; she wants to please them, to meet their expectations. Brie especially wants her father's approval; at the same time she thinks she can't live up to his expectations. "I wanted to be everything he wanted and I couldn't" (*Good Side*, 62). This is an uncomfortable position for all of them. When Brie's judgment goes against what her father wants, Brie feels alienated. She wants to confide in him, but can't. Her father, on the other hand, has to step back and let her make her own mistakes.

Brie's moral development occurs when she takes responsibility for the way she treats others. Brie, like most adolescents, is basically self-centered. She sees people in terms of how they treat her, of how much they like her. When she meets Josh, she wants a boyfriend, someone who is attracted to her. With Kevin, her brother, she wants a knight in shining armor, a priest who can make all her problems go away. And she gets upset when they don't live up to her expectations.

When Josh tells Brie he is a homosexual, she reacts with anger. She says, "The terrible fact of it [Josh's homosexuality] had to be absorbed into everything I did and felt and considered" (*Good Side*, 222). She is only thinking about herself. To her, Josh's homosexuality changes him totally, and she doesn't want to continue to be his friend. She responds in the same way when Kevin confides that he is actually full of self-doubts about his vocation and efficacy as a priest. She even rationalizes lies to her father because if Kevin "could so callously disregard his vows," then nothing mattered (*Good Side*, 90).

Earlier Brie's father had talked about how relationships depend on "commitment after disillusionment." He explained that it's easy to be with people when they are what we want or need; it's a lot more difficult when they don't live up to our expectations. Kevin also understands that the only real choice humans get is "how we react to what life dishes out to us. Are we going to be bitter and hateful or are we going to take what happens and come through with courage and grace?" (Good Side, 248). Brie didn't understand what they were telling her at the time, but now when she is confused about Josh and sick with worry about Kevin, these words come to mind. She knows Josh is the same person she loves, even though he's different than she thought he was. She also sees that failures don't define Kevin as a priest. She sees things from the "good side" of her heart. When Brie helps Kevin take to heart his own words, she thinks, "I was down. I was off that ladder finally. And somehow I knew I'd never be on it again" (*Good Side*,

260). Brie grows up. She has lots of help: her father's words about commitment, her brother's advice to act with charity toward others, and even Josh's knowledge that we can't make people over into something they are not. But in the end, Brie makes the choice to accept others with love.

RINALDI'S THEMES

Rinaldi creates a realistic picture of adolescent girls struggling to grow up in these novels. These girls are trying to form their own identity while struggling with insecurity and lack of self-acceptance. Emotional problems are created by the loss of the mother; in each novel, the mother is either dead or has deserted the family. In *Term Paper*, Nicki feels guilty that she doesn't love her selfish father. Brie has to deal with revelations that shake her view of reality. Sibling relationships are complex as the brother and sister struggle to find the right balance of control and freedom. Not surprisingly, older brothers act as guardians, confidants, and role models. Their occupations—teacher, doctor, priest—put them in advising and nurturing positions. The challenge for the brothers is to see what they have to learn from their younger sisters. The girls deal with insecurity and limited knowledge. They make mistakes and feel guilty and depressed. But they are survivors and they eventually learn about themselves and others. This is part of the process of self-acceptance and forming identity. These adolescent girls learn about the complexity of human behavior and motives, and they use this knowledge to begin to make choices and to act in more independent and loving ways. Rinaldi's themes of learning about reality, making choices, and achieving independence all revolve around the complex adjustments of coming of age for her adolescent characters. These are the themes that will be played against historical facts in her historical fiction novels.

• 3 •

Coming of Age as Americans

*R*inaldi's historical fiction covers a wide variety of events in American history from colonial beginnings through the nineteenth century: the Revolutionary War, the Civil War, the westward movement, and the development of industrialism and the factory system in the United States. Only one novel so far, *Keep Smiling Through*, covers events in the twentieth century, life on the home front during the 1940s and World War II. In all her historical fiction Rinaldi sets out to show the intersections of personal lives with events taking place in the larger context of historical time. Rinaldi accurately presents historical events, but filtered through the eyes and experiences of her adolescent characters. In each novel, an adolescent girl is the central focus of the story. She observes events happening around her and tries to make sense of them, even while these events are shaping and changing her. Rinaldi's characters start out with a naive point of view. They are trying to figure things out, to make choices based on their limited knowledge. As they gain experience, these characters begin to understand more fully the events they are living through as well as themselves, and they begin to change and grow. By connecting her characters' lives with historical events, Rinaldi gives readers a feeling of living through the events. We experience with the characters how it feels to grow in understanding of what it means to live in a particular time.

COMING OF AGE: THE TEENAGE DILEMMA

Rinaldi's fiction is centered on the coming of age of the young heroine. Coming of age, in one form or another, is also the central theme in most young adult novels. Usually the story begins with the character as a child, immature and dependent on family or others. The character is poised to break out of this protective and safe environment to seek new experiences, to take risks, to become self-sufficient. This is a natural stage of adolescence in which the child yearns for independence. Usually this stage leads to a period of struggle between adolescents and their parents or other adults as they try to negotiate the changes that must occur to enable the child to take on adult responsibilities. In many adolescent novels, the child is pushed into this stage even more quickly when parents are eliminated through death, accident, or other circumstances. Suddenly the child must face and meet challenges without the benefit of parental support. This difficult and often harrowing experience becomes a learning and growing time for the child, who must overcome physical and psychological obstacles in order to survive. Mastering difficulties helps the child discover her strengths—her ability and courage—or other qualities of character. The final stage of the coming-of-age process occurs when the child, who has changed in significant ways, is reunited with the family or community. Now the young adult does not return to childish ways but is recognized as a different person, someone who is more mature, more independent, and ready to take on more adult responsibilities.

THE NATION AS ADOLESCENT

Strikingly, this pattern of individual human development parallels the growth of political identity in a nation. Citizens of the United States went through an identity crisis, first as colonists deciding whether to remain loyal or throw off the rule of their home country and second as new Americans discovering what it meant to be an American citizen. The British colonists were expected to defer to the demands and government of the homeland. Laws were imposed and taxes levied that were beneficial to England. The colonists were either ignored or considered secondary to the decision-making process. This precipitated a challenge to the colonists—should they continue to act as dependents with lesser rights or should they demand equal status as citizens? Crisis followed, with England demanding loyalty and obedience and the rebels seeking equality and co-rule. The colonists did not start out wanting to overthrow England and set up their own nation. They developed this point of view through a long period of struggle. It took many years before the colonists discovered that full independence was their goal.

Like an individual person, the colonists came of age as they sought and demanded equality and independence and forged a unique identity.

Rinaldi unites these two strands—the coming-of-age theme in human development and the growth of a unique political identity for the American colonies—in her novels about the Revolutionary War period. In each case the main character, who is an adolescent girl, is going through a personal crisis of struggling with reality. She begins to ask questions and tries to penetrate the surface of events and the motives of other people even as she tries to understand herself. As she learns, she grows in her sense of who she is. This individual process of maturing parallels how the American colonies struggled to define themselves with respect to England.

SARAH'S SECRETS

In *The Secret of Sarah Revere* (1995), Sarah, the thirteen-year-old and second oldest daughter of Paul Revere, is struggling to find the truth about events taking place around her: Who fired the first shot at Lexington? What is the relationship between Rachel, her stepmother, and Doctor Warren? How should she deal with her new feelings for Doctor Warren? Sarah's father calls her his favorite, but she knows that her older sister Debby gets most of the attention.[1] Talking about her place in the family, Sarah says, "My grandmother favors Debby. I think Grandmother hates me a little because I didn't get pox marks. Debby is her favorite, being named after her, you see" (*Secret*, 23). Sarah is the peacemaker in the family. After her mother dies and Debby is running wild, Sarah says, "Things were not good in our house. I knew I must do something to bring Father out of his shell" (Secret, 37). Later when Rachel, Revere's new wife, is unhappy about his political activities, Sarah helps by telling her to talk to Doctor Warren. "He knows everything father is about. . . . I'm sure he'd tell you what you want to know" (*Secret*, 64). Sarah is sensitive and caring, at times more tuned in to others' feelings than her own.

When the novel opens Sarah is troubled not only by the secrets of the family members' involvement in the growing rebellion but also by her personal feelings about Doctor Warren. She doesn't understand why she suddenly wants him to notice her or why she is jealous over Rachel's friendship with him. Most of all Sarah regrets that she accused Warren of being more than just friends with her stepmother. She wants to blame Debby for tricking her into fighting with Warren, but in her heart, Sarah knows this isn't true. She is anxious to sort out her confused feelings and settle her rift with Doctor Warren, but she doesn't have much time to concentrate on her personal problems. Her father, Paul Revere, asks Sarah to deal with the constant visitors who want to hear about events at Lexington and Concord. Ever since the first shots were fired, people have been pestering him to find out which side fired first.

Sarah wonders how to sort things out, how to discover the truth. She asks, "What matters, Father? What's true? Or what people think?" (*Secret*, 8). Is Debby's assessment of Rachel and Warren's relationship true? Is public opinion about who started the war more important than what actually happened? Revere tells her that the truth is what matters, but Sarah wonders how you can know the truth. She decides she has to "put it all together . . . and make sense of it" (*Secret*, 28).

On the afternoon that Sarah sits down in her garden, June 17, 1775, to take time to think about the secrets in her heart, the Revere family is waiting for Doctor Warren before he joins the fighting on Bunker Hill (really Breed's Hill). Warren, a thirty-four-year-old physician and patriot, single-handedly created an American army, after fighting broke out between the British and the militiamen at Lexington. Like Warren, Paul Revere had been "doing things against the king" (*Secret*, 62) for many years, long before he secretly left Boston and rode across the countryside to warn people that British troops were on the march. The rebellious acts of Warren and Revere and countless other colonists have led to open warfare. Congress is about to convene to see if other colonies will join in the fight with the men from Massachusetts. Sarah knows this is a very unsettled time; she says, "Nobody knew the rules . . . for breaking with the mother country or making war. We were on new ground now, making up the rules each morning when we got out of bed" (*Secret*, 14).

TRUTH OF SELF AND TRUTH OF HISTORY

Sarah's emotional state, uncertain and anxious, is like the state of the colonies in 1775, embarking on replacing the traditional political order. Rinaldi uses Sarah's personal turmoil to explore what it felt like to live through these trying times as well as to explore Sarah's process of maturing and dealing with the complexities in her world.

From her immature point of view, Sarah wonders if she will ever understand whether what's true or what people think matters more. She is aware that people have different ideas about what is true, and she wonders if truth is only relative. In the novel Rinaldi shows how Sarah's experiences educate her about the nature of truth. Sarah's father insists that truth matters even when people want to believe their own version of events or their own perceptions. For example, where public opinion wants to place blame on one side, the truth is that both sides, the English and the colonists, were equally involved in starting the war. Revere says, "My God, we're anything but innocent, Sarah. We started this thing as well as they did" (*Secret*, 13). Sarah, also, recalls when people gossiped that Revere "met Rachel in the street outside his shop," but Sarah knows the truth. Sarah and her brother Paul met and liked Rachel and brought her home. Sarah knows Debby was sure there was something wrong with Rachel's friendship with Lady Frankland, wife of a Tory. But when Debby warns that a Tory can't be trusted, her father, Revere, cautions her not to be so sure because people are complex, with ambiguous motives. He says, "Many are confused about the turn things have taken. . . . You know what you are and what you stand for. With some people it is not so simple. Most people don't know how to feel. They have old ties, new concerns, family considerations" (*Secret*, 116). Revere tells Sarah, "What matters is what's true. Always. If we didn't know that, would we thinking men here in Boston do what we're doing to defend our rights? Would they be laying plans in Philadelphia for a congress if they worried what the British think?" (*Secret*, 118).

By comparing "real" truth to subjective truth, Sarah learns that what is real and true should be apparent to people. They often lose sight of reality because it goes against what they want to think. The process of maturing, however, lies in seeing reality as it is and accepting it and living according to it.

Sarah's personal uncertainties mirror the confused opinions and ideas in the colonies about the meaning of the events taking place. Sarah's struggle is to resist being ruled by what other people think and to follow her own head and heart to the truth. Intuitively, she realizes that Rachel's friendship with Warren helps to further the colonial cause because they are passing useful information from the Loyalists to the rebel leaders. But she denies the truth and allows Debby's version of the truth to rule her mind. She isn't mature enough to stick by her own assessment of the situation, and she speaks harsh words to Warren. Even Debby blames Sarah for her behavior. She tells her, "You shouldn't let people tell you what to think. . . . You tricked yourself, Sarah. You think you're so grown-up. . . . Take some advice from me, little sister. Know what you're about. . . . And don't let anyone influence what you think. That's what being grown-up is about, after all" (*Secret*, 173–175).

Sarah realizes the truth of Debby's accusation and decides she will make things right; never again will she allow herself to be overly influenced by other persons' ideas or opinions. Sarah vows to think for herself. As a sign of this new commitment, Sarah offers kindness to Lady Frankland when Debby snubs her, and she decides she must look for the right moment to make her peace with Doctor Warren. She follows her father's advice, "We must all decide, in our hearts, what's true. We must make our own truth every day. And hold it close. And not let anyone take it from us" (*Secret*, 280). Discovering the truth makes Sarah strong and capable of difficult acts.

In Sarah's personal growth and development Rinaldi has created a parallel to the historical situation. Just as Sarah has to decide to follow what she knows to be true, the colonists had to decide to act on what they knew to be true about their need for self-determination. This is what Revere believed the colonists would have to discover for themselves. They had to realize the true nature of their relationship to Britain and decide if they wanted to live as colonists or claim their independence. Revere says, "If we keep what we know as truth in our hearts, it will keep us strong. And bring us through. If we let people take it from us, we are nothing" (*Secret*, 281). This means not allowing public sentiment or politically constructed ideas to interfere with the commitment to seeking the truth. In the end Sarah realizes what her father is telling her. She says, "The real truth is clear, if we choose to see it. But it is also terrifying" (*Secret*, 283). The truth about their relationship to England and their true nature as a people gives the colonists a clear guide to action even though it is difficult. So, too, Sarah faces the truth about her father and Warren. She says, "I knew there was only one truth. And not the truth as we make it for ourselves every day" (*Secret*, 282). Sometimes this truth has to remain unspoken, and sometimes it hurts because we have to recognize how we acted according to false perceptions. Sarah grows up when she understands the truth about her relationship with Doctor Warren. Sarah knows that she is the one who changed, not Warren, who continues to hold her in his affections as a "dear and true friend" (*Secret*, 291). She decides not to mistrust her own judgment. Sarah thinks, "We must make our truths and move on. Or we will never have any peace in our hearts" (*Secret*, 289). This is an important lesson for Sarah—one that was also at the heart of the colonists' commitment to independence.

LOYALTY TO SELF OR COUNTRY

Rinaldi uses a similar pattern in other novels about the Revolutionary War. The main character, an adolescent girl, who is also the naive narrator, goes through a process of education, often leading to her coming of age. Political events affect her while at the same time they mirror her own struggles to understand herself and the people and events around her. In *Time Enough for Drums* (1986), fifteen-year-old Jemima Emerson lives in Trenton, New Jersey, in 1776, when her family and neighbors are trying to figure out their loyalties. Her father becomes a member of the Committee of Safety, charged with commissioning military officers for the Continental Army and scrutinizing the Tories living in Trenton. Her brother David, who is fourteen, is making guns at the local steel mill, and twenty-year-old Dan recruits men to join the fighting. Her mother, under the pen name Intrepid, is writing letters in support of the American Army that are being reprinted in other Patriot newspapers. People are changing like the times and nothing is what it appears.

Jem has a lot to learn about people and their motives. She is quick to make judgments based on superficial appearances. She suspects her tutor John Reid is a Tory sympathizer and spy, despite the fact that he is a trusted friend of her parents and their choice for her tutor. Jem's mother first voices the important theme of the novel when she warns Jem that her reactions to her tutor are wrong. Her mother says, "People are much more than they appear on the outside."[2] Jem's education comes through a series of shocks: realizing that her mother is writing letters that support opposition to the British, which is an act of treason; dealing with the murder of her father by the British; and discovering that John Reid is actually a spy for the Americans. Jem learns that people are more complicated than she thought. For example, she thinks that Reid's attention to elegant clothing reflects an aristocratic point of view that makes him an ally with the Tories. She thinks her mother's sorrow has caused her to retreat from reality, not realizing her deep sense of guilt that she may have caused her husband's death. Later Jem learns firsthand how complex reactions can be when she talks with one of the British officers occupying Trenton. When he reveals his fears about fighting so far from home, she finds herself sympathizing with him even though he represents everything that has destroyed her family. She asks herself, "But how could he be the enemy and be kind? That made less sense than anything" (*Drums*, 180). Jem confronts this same dilemma in trying to deal with her older sister Rebeckah who has married a British officer. Becky criticizes Jem for not acting ladylike, for being "wild," and forgetting "seemly" behavior. But Becky shows not the least feeling for her family. She is intent on caring for her own needs and does not take time to see her mother nor to help Jem with the family business. She fears gossip when Jem wants to nurse Reid when he returns sick from a spying mission. When Becky demands that Jem choose between her or Reid, Jem realizes that she has to do what she knows is right. She decides she can't follow rules that appear to be right on the surface but ignore important truths.

The colonists in this first year of their rebellion against Britain are experiencing chaos while people's loyalties are being questioned. Manners and civility must be maintained to keep society functioning, but they cannot interfere with the difficult choices that have to be made. Jem's father tells her, "The most important thing we're going to have to learn, if we win our freedom in these colonies, is to handle it properly" (*Drums*, 75). While wanting Jem to learn how to be a lady, he also wants her to learn moral clarity. In the end, Jem's mother tells her, "Do what is right. . . . You can learn to live with your decision. That's what you must learn" (*Drums*, 226). The colonists are living this out in their lives as they make the difficult choices and sacrifices to claim the freedom that they know is right. In her personal life Jem goes through a similar struggle.

MISSING PIECES

In *Finishing Becca* (1994), fourteen-year-old Becca Syng serves as a maid to Peggy Shippen, daughter of a prominent Quaker family in Philadelphia, who marries Benedict Arnold. While historians still debate Peggy Shippen's role in Arnold's decision to become a traitor, Rinaldi presents Peggy as an equal partner in her husband's plot to undo the rebel government. It is 1778 and Philadelphia is occupied first by the British and then by the Americans. The British government is offering to work out a peace settlement, while the colonists try to forge a French alliance. Class divisions in society are exaggerated by the fact that many of the well-to-do have sided with the British for business reasons while the common people, who have less to lose, have been more likely to identify themselves with the rebels.

Like many others, Becca has mixed feelings about what the war means to her personally. Her brother serves with Washington and is encamped at Valley Forge, while she has had to fend off marauding Hessians. But in the Shippen household the war seems far away. The Shippens are trying to maintain their neutrality, supporting neither side in the conflict. Becca's mother explains, "Judge Shippen is doing his best to remain neutral. But he has kept open house for General Sir William Howe and his staff since they came here" (*Becca*, 29). So he is being watched by the rebel authorities and has been losing lots of money. His daughter Peggy is enjoying the activities occasioned by the presence of soldiers when she goes out to parties and dances. Peggy has no loyalty to either side; instead she is filled with one ambition—"to be the most popular woman in Philadelphia" (*Becca*, 105).

In any unsettled time, people are confused about which side they support. Some, like the Quakers or the merchants, try to remain neutral. Becca's mother says, "We're waiting, like everyone else, to see what will happen" (*Becca*, 30). Others take advantage of the situation to achieve their own ends. Henry Job, Becca's stepfather, spies for both the British and Americans, having loyalty to neither, in order to get money. Some end up changing sides, perhaps because their loyalty was weak or they want to serve their own ambitions. General Benedict Arnold is criticized for his high style of living, funded, many believe, through speculating on hard-to-find supplies. His behavior leads to accusations that he has Tory leanings and prompts an investigation of his affairs by a military court. Arnold, encouraged by Peggy, becomes a traitor when he feels passed over and unappreciated by his superiors. In the end Becca realizes that material values "had ruined the high-placed and the lowly" (*Becca*, 327).

Becca thinks of herself as a person with "missing pieces" (*Becca*, 32–33) and, at first, thinks manners are what she lacks. She takes the job as Peggy Shippen's maid because her mother sees it as a type of finishing school, a way for Becca to learn the arts, diction, and rules of etiquette of an upper-class lady. But through her experiences in the Shippen household, Becca realizes that social station or wealth isn't important to her. She sees how Peggy uses people, how she has no loyalties, and how she and other girls of her social class indulge in "frivolous pleasures while all around them people were dying for what they believed in" (*Becca*, 139). She learns to "look at things differently. Things that were right in front of us before, we start to see with new eyes" (*Becca*, 251). She realizes that everyone tries to put together his or her missing pieces—she does, as do her stepfather, Peggy Shippen, Benedict Arnold, the colonists. She also realizes, "Some people just look in the wrong places" (*Becca*, 341). Henry Job and Arnold and Becca for a while think that their missing pieces are material things or manners or other people. But what they really need to find are "*parts of ourselves* that we must find and make strong and use to furnish that elegant house inside us" (*Becca*, 326 and 341). In the end Becca, like many of her fellow countrymen and women, discovers character and personal values are more important than anything else.

ROLE MODELS

Another consistent pattern in Rinaldi's novels is the way adolescent girls learn what is true from strong female role models. Since these young girls are trying to learn about themselves and how to act as adults, it's only natural that they look at how other women have made this transition. In *Finishing Becca*, Becca at first looks to Peggy as a model, representing all the gentility and manners and refinement that would make her a lady. But her imitation of Peggy's behavior is short-lived. When Becca meets Peggy's older sister, Elizabeth, who speaks her mind and has independently chosen to aid the rebels, Becca realizes this is the type of woman she wishes to become. Becca says, "Never had I heard a young woman speak with such force and certainty. If I could learn from her, I decided, instead of doing French and needlework, I would certainly find my missing pieces" (*Becca*, 106). The adolescent girls in *The Fifth of March* (1993) and *A Ride into the Morning* (1991) learn from their role models more mature and independent ways of behaving. Rachel Marsh, in *The Fifth of March*, learns from two women, Abigail Adams and another serving girl, Jane Washburn. Mary Cooper, in *A Ride into the Morning*, learns from her cousin, Tempe Wick.

WHAT MARY COOPER
LEARNS IN *A RIDE INTO THE MORNING*

Mary Cooper, at fourteen, is strong-willed and outspoken. She has so alienated her family with her Patriot leanings that they have packed her off to help her cousin Tempe on the Wick family farm in Morristown, New Jersey. It is 1781, the second winter that American troops have wintered at the farm. Mary is excited to be at the farm because it is in the middle of everything. She feels ready to serve the fight for independence in some way. She says, "My mind has been seized by the excitement of this war from the very beginning" (*Morning*, 19). But Mary has an unrealistic view of the glories of war. She sentimentalizes the hungry and cold soldiers and indulges in fantasies about General Wayne as a dashing, romantic figure.

Tempe Wick, at twenty-two, is Mary's older and wiser cousin. Tempe has seen at firsthand the suffering and cost of war. She says, "I've had my fill of this war, Mary. Of that miserable army camped out there, of their wretched women coming to our door begging for scraps of food, and of their wretched children" (*Morning*, 9). Tempe blames the war for breaking her father's heart and leading to his death. She says, "I saw what happened to my father last winter. He couldn't hold himself aloof from what was going on out there. He tore himself in two trying to feed those people and us. It killed him" (*Morning*, 59). With her father and brothers gone, Tempe must run the farm and care for her invalid mother. She has even postponed her marriage in order to fulfill these responsibilities. Torn by her duties as well as a sense that the suffering of the troops is overwhelming, Tempe tries to keep out of the war, not to involve herself in what is happening. She thinks of her choice as a compromise. She can only do so much and she has to get along. This is a pragmatic choice, but in the long run, it's what works. She says, "It'll mean less wear and tear later on" (*Morning*, 59).

Mary is shocked that her cousin doesn't live up to her memories. Mary thinks, "The war has changed her. . . . She is no longer the sweet, generous Tempe I recollect" (*Morning*, 13). She also thinks that Tempe is wrong to talk about compromise. Mary starts out very sure about what she believes and judges Tempe for failing to act according to principles. But soon Mary's romantic notions are tested. She encounters firsthand the suffering of the soldiers and their families when she distributes soup to the hungry people and meets a woman whose child has just died. Mary says, "I was weak with anger and helplessness and torn with guilt. There was not a quiet place left in my soul. . . . This part of the war has nothing to do with the word *freedom,* or how I harken to the sound of it" (*Morning*, 72).

Mary also sees Tempe caught between her compassion for the suffering of the soldiers and their demands that she give concrete support to their cause. The soldiers plan to desert their posts and march to Philadelphia in order to deliver a list of grievances to the Continental Congress. Their organizer, Billy Bowzar, wants to ride Tempe's horse, Colonel, when he leads the mutiny so that the officers will take them more seriously. Worn out by the suffering of the soldiers and fearful of Bowzar's threats against her family, Tempe agrees to give him Colonel. But before it is too late, Tempe realizes that this is not a compromise, but the wrong choice. Wanting to do something, she almost did the wrong thing. Giving her horse to the troops would not only support their cause but could also lead to the end of the revolution. Faced with this realization, Tempe puts herself in danger to elude the soldiers and hides the horse inside the house so they won't be able to find him.

Mary has to see Tempe for what she really is, a confused and angry person. Tempe is neither perfect nor ideal; she is a person who makes mistakes, or even does the right thing, but for the wrong reasons. She is "the sum total of all her experiences" (*Morning,* 101). Seeing Tempe in a more realistic way, Mary realizes what growing up means: "Growing up means that you see the faults of those around you and can no longer hold them above you, unattainable and worshiped from afar" (*Morning*, 160). By witnessing Tempe's conflicts, Mary changes and grows in her understanding of Tempe and herself. Mary tells Tempe, "I'm not as sure of myself as I was when I first came here" (*Morning*, 259). Mary realizes the cost of standing for one's principles. She sees that choices are never just simple decisions and that confusion sets in when people live in difficult times. She tells Tempe, "Living in the middle of an encampment and seeing all the privation can make anyone addlebrained" (*Morning*, 259). Mary learns that people may want to avoid a difficult decision. They may find that compromise works most of the time, but when they come face to face with the truth, they can find the strength and courage to respond. Through Tempe, Mary learns a more realistic view of human behavior.

THE EDUCATION OF
RACHEL MARSH IN *THE FIFTH OF MARCH*

In *The Fifth of March*, Rachel Marsh is an indentured servant, caring for the children of John and Abigail Adams. The family has recently arrived in Boston, a city in turmoil because of the quartering of British troops and the taxes on tea, glass, and paper imposed by the Townsend Acts. Rachel, at fourteen, feels insecure and alone. She is an orphan with only one living relative, an abusive and manipulative uncle. Rachel wants to become someone; she wants to think for herself and become self-sufficient. When asked, she says she wants a "proper dowry" and she needs "to marry and find my place in the world. I want a place of my own" (*March*, 9–10). But she isn't talking just about marriage. Rachel wants to be valued for who she is. She says, "It has to do with the kind of person I want to be. And how I fit in to everything. I want people to listen when I open my mouth. And know I'm worth listening to" (*March*, 10).

Two women, from widely different economic and social stations, provide models for Rachel: Jane Washburn, another indentured servant, and Abigail Adams, a woman "descended from many shining lights in the colony" (*March*, 2). At seventeen Jane has strong opinions about women's roles and the events taking place in Boston. She thinks women have to be serious because soon they too will have a say about politics. She believes that all people, including the common people, should be proud of who they are as they prepare for the "opportunity" that is about to come. Common people will have just as large a role as the gentry in the changes that will come about when there is revolution against British rule. Rachel admires Jane's way of speaking her mind, but she is also afraid of the way Jane talks about staying alert and making choices (*March*, 5). Rachel doesn't want to take sides; she wants to concentrate on bettering herself. She doesn't think that making choices is appropriate for someone in her station. But Jane's convictions teach Rachel. She pushes Rachel to examine her motives and those of others. She also emphasizes commitment to her friends and to her work for the cause of independence. She tells Rachel, "If we gave up now, it would be for nothing" (*March*, 221). Jane thinks Rachel has to face the person she is becoming, "a true American," even when it makes her afraid.

Abigail Adams represents the grace and culture that Rachel believes will help her to become a self-sufficient person. But Rachel fears that Adams' level of education is beyond her capacity because she herself comes from a lower social class. Adams assures Rachel, "We are all born to education. . . . The question is, however, can our society tolerate a woman becoming educated?" (*March*, 34). Adams has enlightened ideas about the benefits of education for both men and women, although she realizes that society dictates certain roles for women and she does not challenge this order. She cautions Rachel, "As a woman you must ofttimes keep your opinions to yourself in the company of men" (*March*, 36). Adams also tells Rachel that all people are eventually faced with making choices. In the case of Adams and her husband, they have tried to remain neutral but now they are being forced to choose sides. She says, "But sooner or later, it seems, one must declare one's self. If one is to be true to one's self at all" (*March*, 50). These are powerful ideas, and as Rachel observes the behavior of Abigail Adams and her husband, reads books, and recognizes the value of friends as part of the new order of things, she eventually has the courage to stand up for what she knows is right.

Rachel meets and befriends a young British soldier, Private Matthew Kilroy, a sentry stationed outside the Adamses' home. At first she shares food and conversation with him, and in time they begin "walking out" with each other. Matthew wants an even more intimate relationship; however, Rachel only wants to be friends. She tells him her dreams. "That I want us to be friends. That I want no harm to come to you. That I want us to help one another and not let these silly arguments tear us apart" (*March*, 187).

Rachel is true to her friend and also to her knowledge about what really happened on the night of the Boston Massacre. Matthew is one of the soldiers who fired on a crowd of citizens, killing four and wounding others, on March 5, 1770. When he is imprisoned and put on trial for murder, Rachel asks Mr. Adams to serve as his lawyer. She also wants to testify about what she witnessed because she knows the truth. She tells Mrs. Adams, "And I saw what happened. And it wasn't like Mr. Revere's engraving. And if he's sold hundreds, and it's going to be printed in the *Gazette*, then people will think that's how it was" (*March*, 238). Rachel believes that she has the right to speak and that her studies have prepared her to choose the right words so that people will listen. She says, "It's the reason I've studied so hard. So people would listen to me when I spoke. . . . because I've something to say and I know how to say it" (*March*, 239). Rachel follows the example and advice of both Abigail Adams and Jane when she makes her decision to defend Matthew, even though she knows it could cost her the trust of the Adamses and her position in their household. But she makes this choice because she has new ideas about liberty. Liberty is "the right to make up your own mind about things, to decide for yourself what course of action you are going to take. And then follow it" (*March*, 254).

Her decisions to stand by Matthew and to leave the Adamses' household without anger are signs of her new maturity. Rachel learns that character is not limited to a certain social class. Character has to do with making sacrifices, "with thinking of another's feelings before one's own" (*March*, 309). Rachel says, "I knew now that you could grow strong and straight inside even if you never had nine straight-backed cherry chairs in your parlor. . . . even if you lived in a rude sod hut in the wilderness" (*March*, 303–304). This is also the reason Rachel does not take any of the dowry the Adams have put together for her. She wants them to know what kind of person she is, that she is like them, that she can take care of herself and stand on her own. Rachel tells her Uncle Eb, "I have become a plain American. A true American. I know now what I am and what I'm about. I know how to make choices and speak for myself. And I like that feeling. And for the first time in my life, I know I have found a place" (*March*, 319).

Rachel Marsh could be speaking for all the young women in these novels about the coming of age of the colonists as American citizens. These young women are learning lessons about what is true and who they are. They are growing as independent people who make choices based on truth. They, and their nation, are coming of age.

· 4 ·

Confronting Conflicting Values

*I*n the novels about the Revolutionary War in America, the central theme is appearance versus reality, with the historical events mirroring the individual's personal crisis of coming to learn what is true and real. Rinaldi explores another aspect of the coming-of-age theme in other historical novels that concentrate on the adolescent confronting and making difficult moral choices. Again the individual's development is set within a larger social context where a whole group of people faces a moral dilemma, such as the Puritans dealing with accusations of witchcraft in Salem in the late seventeenth century or Southerners facing the moral dilemma of the practice of slavery. Rinaldi fashions the story in similar ways in each novel dealing with this theme. The adolescent girl follows the rules and norms of society, but as her knowledge grows, she naturally begins to question these values. In this process she discovers that evil or social injustice or ignorance have corrupted her community's values. This creates a moral dilemma, with the young girl having to decide whether to act according to her knowledge of what is right or accept things as they are. In making choices that go against the status quo, the character risks losing the security of family, friends, and social group. But not making a choice is equally difficult since it leads to feelings of guilt. However, resolving this conflict and making the difficult choice to do what she thinks is right has the potential to push the protagonist toward greater maturity; otherwise, she retreats from the challenge, remaining in a childish state. In returning to this theme over the years, Rinaldi shows how individuals who decide to do what is right, even when it puts them in conflict with the community, have the potential to become agents of social change.

SEEING WITH NEW EYES

In *The Last Silk Dress* (1988), her second work of historical fiction, Rinaldi creates a rather straightforward view of moral choice. The main character, Susan, starts out as unreflective and naive about the values of her community. She thinks of herself as a Southerner who is dedicated to the Southern Cause. But experiences teach her the truth about slavery, an unjust and corrupt system, and the injustice of fighting to protect this system. With this new knowledge, Susan rejects the Cause and acts decisively to break with her former set of values. In the end she suffers consequences for her action but knows she has done the right thing.

The novel begins on July 21, 1861, as people in Richmond are awaiting news about the Battle of Manassas. Susan Chilmark supports "the Cause" of the South wholeheartedly and wants to do something dramatic to show her loyalty. She believes the South is fighting for its fundamental freedoms, and she admires the bravery and valor of its soldiers. She tells her brother, "The soldiers are all so brave. They'd left their homes to come to Richmond and defend the Confederacy. . . . what we're doing is no different than what the rebels did in 1776. We're not allowing the North to push us around and tell us how to live" (*Dress*, 46). She does what she can to help the Cause: she tends wounded soldiers, she sews flags for the army, and when she realizes that the South does not have a spy balloon, she volunteers to collect silk dresses that can be fashioned into a balloon. Susan is thrilled by the idea of a balloon "made of silk dresses donated by women of the Confederacy!" (*Dress*, 122) that will be able to do reconnaissance missions over Northern lines.

But all the time Susan is working so hard, she is also having experiences that cause her to question the Cause she supports. She is reunited with her "black sheep" brother, Lucien, who refuses to fight for the Confederacy. For the first time, Susan hears someone talk against the South. In fact, Lucien bluntly says, "The Cause stinks. The South has turned lunatic. It has too many long-winded orators who got carried away with themselves and now everyone has to pay for their words. The system is evil and corrupt and they're defending it" (*Dress*, 46). Susan has never really thought about what slavery means, either to the blacks or the slave owners. She is shocked to learn that slaves in her home were bought by her father at a slave auction. Susan also learns that Lucien fell in love with Sallie, one of the slaves in the family, when he was a young man. He even taught Sallie to read, which was illegal and considered dangerous by Southern slave owners. When this was discovered, Lucien's father, Hugh, shipped Sallie North at his wife's insistence. Again Lucien gives Susan something to think about. He tells her, "An affair would have been forgiven. Half the men in the South have nigra mistresses. Love was something else. It could not be forgiven" (*Dress*, 55). Lucien still regrets that he didn't tell his father his true feelings for Sallie and that he couldn't protect her. Hearing Lucien's story, Susan begins to understand her father's sadness and guilt.

When Susan helps tend the wounded, a young soldier dies, and she questions if the Cause is worth his loss. She says, "I wondered why this young boy had to die. And for what? The Cause? It had such a sweet ring to it when people were shouting and marching or discussing it at parties, but here in this silent room it meant nothing to me at all" (*Dress*, 88). Later she thinks of this moment as a turning point. "Before that I was sure about everything. But when that young soldier died I wasn't sure about anything any more. I had only questions I couldn't answer" (*Dress*, 165). Susan eventually comes to identify this feeling of confusion with the process of growing up. She realizes that experience leads to questions and actions have consequences. In fact every action means a person has made a choice even when they aren't aware that they are making a choice. She thinks about what she has been doing, working for the Cause, and how she has to decide what she really believes.

Learning about her family's secrets and her own past shows Susan the direction to take. She learns about the abuses of slavery and its terrible impact on her family. Before she was born, her father had an affair and a child with a slave mistress. Her mother later discovers that Sallie is actually Hugh's child. To get back at him, she has an affair with a Yankee, who is Susan's real father. Susan's mother says, "The true Southern woman is not supposed to let such things bother her. We are supposed to look the other way. . . . Our marriage was never the same when I found out" (*Dress*, 231–232). Susan realizes Lucien left the family when he learned that the woman he loved was really his half sister. She feels "dirty and corrupt and evil" hearing the truth about how slaves were abused. The Southern Cause now seems to be something to be ashamed of rather than honored. Her past seems unreal and the war stupid. She tells her brother, "Those guns never stop. And I don't know what they're for. . . . You were right about the Cause being corrupt and evil. What Daddy did with Lettie . . . that was corrupt" (*Dress*, 254). Susan still loves her father, although she condemns his behavior, and for the first time, she understands her mother's bitterness and anger. She realizes the impact of slavery on her own family and, by extension on all of the South, and regrets the lives lost fighting to support a corrupt system. Lucien puts her thoughts into words: It's "like a house of cards . . . and it's going down. . . . Our brave boys are out there trying to save it. But it will collapse eventually. I get angry at the waste of lives" (*Dress*, 256).

Knowledge propels Susan from innocence to experience. She no longer believes in the Cause but feels caught between what she once was and what she now is. She tells Tim, a Yankee friend of Lucien's and the man she loves, "One minute I hate the South and my own daddy for what he did. . . . And the next minute I'm crying because Daddy's dead. I want things to be the way they were before the war. But I know the way things were then wasn't right, either" (*Dress*, 273). She decides that she has to destroy the balloon, the symbol of all she worked for once, in order to get rid of the past and show her rejection of Southern values. But in order to do this, she has to disobey her brother, who fears for her safety. She decides to act according to her convictions. She remembers what her father told her: "You must always do what is right. That's not an easy charge I'm giving you. As I told you before, there comes a time when the two don't coincide, when doing right means going against those we love" (*Dress*, 103).

Susan's action also leads Lucien to make a commitment. He realizes that he is finally striking out at the South when he shoots a soldier who threatens Susan on the riverbank the night the Confederate balloon is destroyed. Both Lucien and Susan make moral choices by rejecting the South's commitment to slavery. When they act according to justice, Susan and Lucien feel at peace and have a sense of hope. They know that judging what is right is the first step toward beginning to heal in their personal lives and for the South. While they have to leave the South for awhile, they both plan to return to participate in rebuilding the South they love according to a more just and moral order.

THE DIFFICULTY OF MORAL CHOICE

In *A Break with Charity* (1992), Susanna English does what is right, but only after a long period of hesitation. She, like Susan, is happy about her choice, but she feels guilty about the outcome. Susanna is fourteen when she begins to question the way people are acting in Salem, Massachusetts, a predominately Puritan community in 1691. Susanna knows the main tenets of the "Puritan code": "The Puritan virtues are very plain. They are hard work, cleanliness, orderliness of mind and manner, perseverance, courage, piety, a knowledge of one's sins, a desire for forgiveness, hatred for the Devil and all his works, obedience to the clergy, and impatience with heathens."[1] However, it is a difficult time for the community: "what with a recent outbreak

of smallpox, Indian raids on the fringes of the town, and the devout predict-
ing that Doomsday was upon us" (*Charity*, 6). Salem, whose name means
"City of Peace," is actually full of hate. Tituba, the West Indian slave of Reverend Parris, predicts a dark time for the village. She says, "Everything is sin-
ful to these people. They think love is a sin. All they speak of is the Devil.
Tituba knows that if you speak of the Devil enough he will come 'round"
(*Charity*, 22). Intolerance and hatred are undermining the positive values of
the Puritan way. Members of the community who are poor or without pro-
tection are ostracized just because they are different. People want someone to
blame for their disasters. Ann Putnam, leader of the girls who accuse townspeople of being witches, says she is giving the community what it wants. She
tells Susanna, "There is so much evil in this town. . . . the elders will be glad
to know that the cause of the bickering and trouble in this place lies not at
their own feet but is the fault of witches living amongst us" (*Charity*, 73). Ann
is actually the instrument of her mother who wants revenge on her enemies.
But the ministers give her power by listening to her accusations. She says,
"We can name anyone. The power has been given to us by the ministers
themselves. They anxiously look to us for the names" (*Charity*, 76).

Susanna English lives according to Puritan rules, but she is also at the
age when she begins to question them. She describes herself as "not a proper
Puritan." She realizes that she has been influenced by her father's enlightened
ideals. She questions how the Puritans control every aspect of life. But most
of all she questions the idea of being born depraved, already subject to eter-
nal damnation just by being born. When she voices these troubling ideas, her
father is not angry. He identifies her questioning as an aspect of his own re-
ligious tolerance. He says, "I often wonder why our ministers and magistrates
don't consider one fact. Which is that the same spirit that brought us here,
for whatever diverse reasons, can make us splinter this colony into individual hotbeds of freedom if they suffocate us with their claims of superior ho-
liness" (*Charity*, 42).

Because of her education and experiences, Susanna is different from
other Puritan girls in the village. She is allowed to read all the books in her
father's library and encouraged to question authority and think for herself.
Her father is also a merchant, and the family has a higher standard of living
than many others, enabling Susanna to indulge in simple pleasures. Susanna
has traveled to Boston and Virginia and dreams of making voyages to faraway
places on her father's ships just like her brother William.

Some of Susanna's questioning of Puritan rules stems from her dissatis-
factions with dictates against pleasant diversions or physical sensations.
Susanna, at first, thinks that she is the only one with these feelings, until she

talks to the girls who have formed a circle around Tituba and realizes they feel the same dissatisfaction. But where Susanna can explore her ideas with her father who is benevolent and tolerant, other girls in the village do not have similar opportunities. Their repression eventually takes a dangerous outlet. The girls who meet at the home of Reverend Parris seek only a diversion, a way to relieve dreary winter days. Susanna knows that the circle of girls, from which she is excluded, engage in fortune-telling, reading palms, and "little sorceries." She also knows from her own experience that they feel guilty and fear being discovered. She, too, has asked Tituba to read her palm to learn when her brother will return from his sea voyage. Susanna also realizes that Reverend Parris does not know what has been going on in his home, "or he would be meting out punishment, stern man that he was, and not calling in other ministers to pray over the girls" (*Charity*, 66). Knowing what is really happening, Susanna asks Ann Putnam to tell the truth. She says, "But the doctor's verdict about the evil hand being on Abigail Williams and little Betty Parris is not true. We both know such. Someone must say speak out now, before the matter is out of hand" (*Charity*, 72). Ann, however, enjoys the attention, freedom from duties, and power that have come to her and the circle of girls. She refuses to tell the truth.

Susanna's knowledge of the girls' true motives for naming witches in the community and Ann's threats against Susanna's family create a moral dilemma for her. She knows the truth but she is afraid to tell anyone. At first she doesn't speak out because she also feels guilty for having consulted Tituba and for lying to her family. Then she thinks that the girls will stop or the community won't believe them. Susanna hopes that someone else will speak up, maybe Tituba or Mary Warren. She feels paralyzed: "There was nothing I could do now, even if I had a mind to. Anyone who spoke out against them was named or had someone in their family cried out on" (*Charity*, 112). Her mother is accused of witchcraft, but Susanna still fears what could happen to the rest of her family. When her father is also accused of being a witch, the family goes to the jail in Boston, but Susanna stays behind, hoping for a "right time" to tell the truth. Susanna says, "I was the cause of this mayhem and fury in Salem, after all. As much as the demented girls. For they now believed their own lies. I knew them to be untruths. And I might still get the opportunity to speak out if I stayed" (*Charity*, 144). When the hangings begin, Susanna is tormented by both her need to tell and also her fears. Finally, sick at heart when five more women are hanged, Susanna tells what she knows to Joseph Putnam, a member of the community who has been quietly building support against the witch trials.

Even then Susanna wavers. When Mary Bradbury is accused of being a witch who harms sailors, Susanna fears for her brother's safety. She gives in to irrational fears. If it means saving her brother, she wants Mary Bradbury to be hanged as a witch. She realizes, "It was so easy to be drawn into it [believing in witches] when one of your own was threatened!" (*Charity*, 201). Her friend, Johnathan, arranges for her to meet and talk with Mary. Then Susanna sees she is really a wise and kindly person, and Susanna is able to overcome her fears and tell the truth.

In this novel Rinaldi shows that making a moral decision is not a simple action. Susanna's decision is mixed up with ambivalence, guilt, and fear. But her choice is important. Without her testimony, the tide of the witch craze would have taken even longer to stop. Reverend Pike, who takes her testimony, says, "I would not have put pen to paper today had this young girl not told me her tale" (*Charity*, 223). Susanna knows that her speaking out is the right thing to do, but mixed with her good feelings are feelings of guilt, self-recriminations that she should have spoken up sooner.

Susanna is unable to truly forgive herself until she also forgives Ann Putnam, the person she blames for the madness in Salem. To show this Rinaldi frames the events of the novel by a prologue and epilogue set fourteen years later, in 1706. Susanna returns to the Meeting House in Salem Village to witness Ann Putnam's plea for forgiveness. When Susanna recognizes Ann's human weakness and forgives her, she also feels cleansed and ready for healing to begin. Susanna realizes that this is also the Puritan way, "the sealing ordinances of the covenant of grace and church communion." The community is called on to live up to its covenant with God, to forgive the sinner and let the powers of goodness rule. In the end Susanna English is a Puritan woman, who knows the power of evil, but also the power of goodness. As an adolescent Susanna makes a difficult moral choice, and now as an adult she chooses to forgive both the sinner and also herself. Through her knowledge and action, Susanna challenges the community's rules while, at the same time, participating in its promise of moral order.

SHADES OF GRAY

Kay, the main character in *Keep Smiling Through* (1996), learns that a simplistic moral code isn't sufficient to deal with the complexity of events and people. Kay is faced with a moral dilemma, which at first seems to be black and white, with no ambiguity. Instead she learns that there is nothing simple about any of the choices we make to do the right thing. For this novel, Rinaldi draws on her own experiences as a child growing up during World War II to create the story of Kay and her family. The setting in the 1940s, with the threat of attack and the feeling of wartime panic, fits the confusion in the mind of Kay, who wants the comfort of clear-cut realities.

Kay, at ten, growing up in a large family in New Jersey, has never had to make any important decisions. Most of the time people don't listen to her and just ignore her. She is good at making herself invisible. She says, "All I had to do was sit very still and quiet and before I knew it, grown-ups forgot I even existed" (*Smiling*, 13). There is a lot of tension in Kay's family, both because of the difficult economic conditions of rationing and wartime shortages and also because of the harshness of their stepmother. Grace, who is expecting a baby, is demanding and strict. She also doesn't want her husband or stepchildren to mention their dead wife and mother. Even at ten Kay resents this and knows it's what makes her family so upset. She says, "I didn't have to think much to know why we were confused. It was because we'd lost our mother. But not only that, we were never allowed to speak of her. It made Amazing Grace crazy if anyone so much as mentioned her name. There were no pictures of her around anywhere" (*Smiling*, 54–55).

At ten Kay believes in the moral code of the radio heroes of the day. They taught "that all you have to do is stand up for truth and have an unswerving sense of justice and you will be rewarded in the end" (*Smiling*, 1). Whenever Kay is trying to decide what she should do, she relies on their code of behavior. She thinks, "The Lone Ranger is tough and hard, with an iron will and an unswerving sense of justice. . . . Everything would be all right when he got finished" (*Smiling*, 52–53).

But Kay learns "that you can be good and do the right thing and sometimes it all goes bad for you anyway" (*Smiling*, 1). Her grandfather, her stepmother's father, visits an old friend, Ernie, who is a member of the Bund, the American Nazi Party. They are attacked by several men who accuse them of being German sympathizers. Kay finds and hides one of Ernie's pamphlets filled with "Nazi propaganda." She says, "I sensed the pamphlet was everything that the war was all about, that it was a dangerous piece of paper. . . . I needed powers and abilities far beyond those of mortal men, like Superman's, to know what was to be done with it" (*Smiling*, 114).

When the local newspaper decides to do a story on the attack, Kay decides to "do the right thing." She says, "I told them everything. I told them all I knew. . . . I told them the whole truth. . . . But I didn't forget about justice either" (*Smiling*, 141). She defends her grandfather, saying he didn't know what was in the pamphlet. Her stepmother is embarrassed and angry and beats Kay for telling the truth. Kay, who had promised herself that she would be brave, can't stand up to Grace's beating. Kay says, "The good feeling I'd had about doing right was gone" (*Smiling*, 145–146).

Kay's moral code is shaken. Now the world seems "full of treachery, evil, and betrayal" (*Smiling*, 147). She feels guilty when Grace loses her baby, who is born prematurely: "A hundred times in the next week I wished I hadn't told the truth to that reporter and gotten Amazing Grace so upset that she'd had her baby too early" (*Smiling*, 165–166). And even though she hates Grace for hitting her, she sympathizes with Grace who is in a severe depression over the loss of her baby. Then she learns from her best friend that the doctors had to take the baby out of the incubator too soon because of wartime shortages. They had to use the incubator for another baby and they had to choose which baby needed it more. Kay sees that no choices are simple or clear-cut; things don't always work out like in the radio programs. Bad things happen and justice isn't rewarded. This knowledge helps Kay deal with her guilt, although she knows she will always feel a little guilty. She realizes she needs a better way of looking at the world, a way of dealing with ambiguities. As a sign of her maturing, Kay gives up her only baby doll, Mary Frances, to the war effort. Kay thinks, "She understood, if dolls can understand. I know she did. She just kept smiling, smiling right through" (*Smiling*, 186). Kay knows she will continue to do what is right, but not because she expects a reward and not because everything will be right. She will just do the best that she can—she will "keep smiling through."

THE DEATH OF MISS MUFFET

Like Kay, Emily Pigbush, in *An Acquaintance with Darkness* (1997), starts out as naive about reality. She tries to apply simple moral rules, until her experiences in the chaos and disillusionment at the end of the Civil War teach her about the ambiguous nature of reality and moral judgments. While losing her innocent approach to life, Emily begins to realize that she is growing up and developing a more mature way to judge right and wrong. This realization ultimately gives her a feeling of hope that she is coming to see reality in more complex ways.

By 1865 in the city of Washington, many question the terrible toll of the Civil War and the worthiness of "the Cause." Both Northerners and Southerners, claiming right is on their side, engage in violent acts against each other. Emily, who is fourteen and caring for her sickly mother, is worn out by the confusion. "Booth [John Wilkes] was pure Secesh, loved the

South. So did all the Surratts [her friends]. So did half the people in Washington. Mrs. Lincoln herself had had four brothers fighting for the Confederacy. You couldn't sort things like that out anymore."[2] Emily no longer cares about causes. Her beloved father died fighting against the South, but all Emily feels is the terrible loss. Emily's mother is bitter, not that the South is dying, but because she isn't able to live as a Southern belle. Emily says, "She just wanted to play the part, be taken care of by everybody, have Negroes waiting on her" (Darkness, 30). No one is the same, because of the war. Emily's childhood friend and the boy she idolizes, Johnny Surratt, is a different person. He sneaks around, is gone for long periods of time, and refuses to be responsible to others. Her mother fights constantly with her brother, Valentine, who is a respected physician, and hints that he is involved in some terrible activity.

Emily tries to sort out these confusing issues, but she doesn't have a way to deal with moral ambiguity. She says her father taught her "all life's important lessons from fairy tales and nursery rhymes" (*Darkness*, 2). Persons and events are either good or evil. Emily says, "Here in Washington I'd already applied much of what he'd taught me. I had to. All kinds of unsavory people walked the streets . . . and now it seemed like every other person was a stranger, an interloper, an outlander who had come to prey on us" (*Darkness*, 2).

Almost everyone advises Emily about the ambiguous nature of reality. Uncle Valentine urges Emily to think for herself and not let her mother's fears control her. In his experience he has found that people aren't always what you expect; they can be less or more. Marietta, a slave and one-eighth Negro, talks about experiences that drove her to despair and attempted suicide before she was saved by Uncle Valentine. Now she has a philosophy that accepts the bad along with the good. Marietta tells Emily, "So much bad has happened to me. I look at it like fertilizer in a garden. It has helped my soul to grow" (*Darkness*, 73). A family friend and free black woman, Elizabeth Keckley, advises Emily that people are full of contradictions, and "we all, at some time in our lives, have an acquaintance with darkness" (*Darkness*, 17). All of these people are telling Emily that deciding what is right or wrong is complicated and ambiguous.

In this confused state, Emily has to deal with two dilemmas. She has to decide how to judge Johnny, who is named a co-conspirator in the plot with John Wilkes Booth to assassinate President Lincoln. Johnny hides, leaving his mother and sister defenseless. Emily hopes that he isn't a coward and will come forward. She also has to judge Uncle Valentine, her guardian, when she learns he is being investigated by the police. She wonders whether her uncle is an esteemed scientist or a grave robber.

Emily wants to believe in Johnny Surratt and does not condemn him for playing a role in the conspiracy to kill Lincoln. Instead Emily is bothered that Johnny doesn't turn himself in to save his mother. At first she thinks he may not know what is going on; then she receives a letter from Johnny in which he says he is waiting until his mother is in "real danger." Emily defends Johnny to his sister, who says, "It'd help to know Johnny cared enough to come home and put himself in the line of fire for Mama" (*Darkness*, 175). But finally when Mrs. Surratt is brought to trial and sentenced to be hanged, Emily realizes Johnny is weak and cowardly. She thinks, "*Where are you Johnny? If you'd come back they wouldn't be hanging your mother. Couldn't you have come back?*" (*Darkness*, 277). Emily feels a great sense of loss when her romantic notions about Johnny's heroism and courtliness are broken.

Likewise, with her uncle's work it isn't the grave robbing that ultimately bothers Emily, but being betrayed by those she trusts. Her father taught her not to "enter into difficult arrangements to save the moment," (*Darkness*, 144), which is what Emily feels she has done. She has accepted the comfort of her uncle's home without knowing what he is doing. She decides she has to know whether her uncle is engaged in stealing bodies or not, "For my own sanity . . . if I wanted to live in peace with myself" (*Darkness*, 146). When Emily searches her uncle's lab with his assistant Robert and finds barrels labeled pickles, instinctively she realizes something else is in the barrels. She thinks, "But I was sure whatever was in them was for the good of mankind. Perhaps some new discovery. Who was I to question it?" (*Darkness*, 156).

Even though she wants to believe in her uncle, Emily continues to feel ambivalent about him. "It was all starting to add up, and I did not like the arithmetic. Then the next minute I would look around me at the ordered rhythms of the house, at Uncle Valentine's casual and yet elegant demeanor; I would think of the good he was doing, and know I was wrong" (*Darkness*, 187). As Emily witnesses her uncle's dedication to scientific research and his unselfish risks to help his patients, she begins to ask herself, "Were there degrees of right and wrong?" (*Darkness*, 192). When her friend asks, "What's so bad about what your uncle has done? How do you think doctors got to know everything they now know?" (*Darkness*, 220), Emily realizes that she does not think body snatching is wrong. Rather she resents that her uncle is lying to her. Emily wants to blame her uncle and his assistant Robert for not telling her the truth, but they both hold her to account, too. Her uncle says, "You have suspected the true nature of my work all along, haven't you. . . . Then why didn't you ask me outright?" (*Darkness*, 242). Also Emily "interfered" with medical science by releasing Addie, a patient in her uncle's home, before her cure was completed. Her uncle considers this act worse than anything he has done. Emily can't defend herself or fall back on a simple way of judging right and wrong. Now in her own situation, she sees the complex and ambiguous nature of her actions.

Emily feels guilty for her actions when she thought she was doing the right thing. She also tries to make amends for interfering with her uncle's scientific work by claiming a dead body from the Almshouse, but knows she will probably feel the need to do some "additional penance for the loss of Addie" for the rest of her life. Emily's view of the world changes through her experiences. In the end when she attends the hangings of the Lincoln conspirators, including Johnny Surratt's mother, Emily says, "And I knew I could never be the way I had been before. None of us could. Miss Muffet was dead. My daddy was dead. The world as we had all known it before the war and the shooting of Lincoln, that innocent world, was dead. This was the world now, as we had brought it upon ourselves to be" (*Darkness*, 279). But mixed with Emily's sense of loss and guilt is a feeling of hope that her new knowledge will enable her to see things in more complex ways.

Rinaldi uses the historical situation in each novel to show the complexity of reality, and she explores the development of moral understanding through the choices of each of these characters. For Susan in *The Last Silk Dress* there are no barriers to moral choice. Once her eyes are opened, she acts decisively to do the right thing. The other characters have a much more difficult time acting on their knowledge. They feel guilt and responsibility and see the world as a complicated, often ambiguous, place where clear-cut decisions are difficult to make. But they also mature as they learn to accept themselves and cope with reality. They learn that rules won't fit every situation. Instead they begin to formulate a way of looking at the world that allows for the complexity of human motives and choices.

• 5 •

Forging Individual Identity

"$\mathcal{W}$ho am I?" is the fundamental question of adolescence and the coming-of-age theme in literature. Children naturally question who they are, both as individuals and also as members of a family, peer group, and racial or cultural group, with their questions increasing during the teen years. Identity as a part of coming of age is an important theme to Rinaldi for personal reasons as well as from a storyteller's point of view. Rinaldi experienced the effects of an identity crisis when she was growing up because she knew very little about her mother. In the author's note to *Wolf by the Ears*, Rinaldi writes, "My own mother had died when I was born. . . . So there was always a part of me I could not acknowledge, a part of me I yearned to understand" (*Wolf*, x). Rinaldi also met other people with this problem. When she was a newspaper columnist, she met people who claimed to be the Lindbergh baby, and she saw the alienation, confusion, and personal cost of not knowing one's identity. Thus, as a storyteller, Rinaldi recognized the inherent conflict facing people who discover things about themselves that they did not know or who are caught between two different identities. Stories about how an individual resolves this conflict hold important truths for a storyteller. So over the years, Rinaldi looked for "a real figure in American history to write about in connection with alienation" (*Wolf*, x). In several novels dealing with the complex historical relationship of blacks and whites and the issue of slavery in the United States, Rinaldi found the vehicle to explore the dilemma of not knowing one's true identity and creating a new identity for oneself.

SEARCHING FOR THE FATHER

The question of identity is set before the reader in the opening pages of *Wolf by the Ears* (1991), a novel written as the journal of Harriet Hemings, nineteen-year-old daughter of Sally Hemings, the slave mistress of Thomas Jefferson. Harriet describes herself as "a nigra servant" but immediately says two contradictory things. She says she is actually a slave. Then she writes, "Yet I feel that I am more. I know I am more" (*Wolf*, 9–10). This conflict within Harriet is represented by her choice whether or not to leave Monticello when she reaches twenty-one. Jefferson has promised Sally Hemings that he would free her children when they came of age.

Harriet identifies herself as a black woman who lives in a world separate from "white folks." Yet Jefferson's attention to her needs, her sense of his position as a great and benevolent man, and especially her belief that Jefferson is her real father—all give Harriet a sense that she is a unique individual who cannot be defined solely by her condition as a slave. Harriet's education about her identity takes place throughout the rest of the novel. Harriet has to recognize what it truly means to be a slave. Thomas Mann Randolph, son-in-law of Jefferson and governor of Virginia, reminds Harriet that "kindness is not freedom. And security is not freedom" (*Wolf*, 28). He realizes Harriet confuses her love for Jefferson with an acceptance of an inferior status. He tells her that, like her, many people are confused about the nature of slavery. Jefferson himself calls slavery "a wolf America has by the ears. And that we can no longer hold onto it. But neither can we let it go" (*Wolf*, 29).

Harriet also considers her decision in the light of what she sees happening to her brother, Beverly. He is twenty-two but has not taken his freedom, because he hopes Jefferson will send him to the university. Jefferson refuses, saying he cannot go against the "unwritten rules of society" and "the way of things" (*Wolf*, 44). When Harriet overhears their conversation, she realizes the futility of Beverly's hope that Jefferson will recognize him as a son and treat him as he would his own children. Beverly is caught in the "velvet trap of the master's love" (*Wolf*, 46), living a lie that will eventually destroy him. Seeing Beverly's situation helps Harriet realize how important it is for her to leave Monticello.

Then Harriet begins to understand how much her mother values freedom. Harriet discovers that her mother has been sewing fine clothes for her to wear when she leaves the plantation. Sally Hemings wants her children to have freedom, more than anything, even though she will never see them again once they leave.

The turning point for Harriet comes when she is physically attacked by Charles Bankhead, husband of Jefferson's granddaughter Anne. Harriet realizes that she is nothing more than a slave to this man and others, and as a marriageable young woman she is vulnerable if she doesn't leave Monticello. Also she realizes that if Jefferson died before she came of age, she could be sold. The possibility of being identified solely as a slave, a status that would deny all the complicated knowledge she has about who she is, compels Harriet to choose freedom.

But there is a second question for Harriet: she also has the choice of renouncing her identity as a black woman in order to have an easier time in the white world. Randolph tells Harriet that passing "would make the difference between having a good life and struggling" (*Wolf,* 106). For Harriet this is an impossible decision. It means "giving up everything I am" (*Wolf,* 107) and turning her back on her people. Again her mother urges Harriet to make this choice because "freedom is worth everything. There is no sacrifice too great" (*Wolf,* 115). Her mother also tells Harriet that her older brother Tom made the decision to pass as a white person. Sally believes that the present sacrifice may have rich results in time. She says, "Who knows what his children will accomplish someday. . . . And they will know who they are" (*Wolf,* 114).

For two years, Harriet studies with Martha, Jefferson's daughter, in order to prepare for her life as a white woman. Harriet thinks, "Going into a white world. No more nigra servant. What is it like to be a white lady? Suppose I can't do it? Suppose people find out? How will I ever stop being me—Harriet Hemings from Monticello, whose mama is Sally Hemings?" (*Wolf,* 174). Harriet has new clothes, sewn by her mother, and she will take a new name, Elizabeth Lackland. She is also betrothed to a white man in order to prevent a forced marriage to one of Jefferson's slaves before she leaves Monticello. But there are two major issues that Harriet has to resolve: Who is her father, and what happens to Harriet Hemings when she takes a new name?

Harriet does not know if Jefferson is really her father. She thinks he is because of the way he treats her and her brothers, but she does not know for sure. Also Martha Jefferson tells Harriet that her real father is Peter Carr, Jefferson's nephew, who spent some time at Monticello around the time of her birth. Not knowing creates confusion for Harriet. She tells Beverly, "There's days I know I'm nigra, and what's mine is in those cabins down there. Days when I know it so much that I hate myself for wanting to leave, let alone pass! Then, other times I know I'm different. There's times I *want* more, Bev. Times I know I *deserve* more! Because of who I am. And then I feel so guilty about it" (Wolf, 142). Harriet feels caught between her two selves, her self as a black woman and slave and her self as the child of Jefferson. She wonders how she can leave Jefferson, "the tall, kind man who rides his horse like a god and who puts his arm around me and tells me stories of Mama when she was a girl" (Wolf, 32). She wonders if she would have the expectations that she has if she didn't think Jefferson was her father. Beverly understands Harriet's dilemma because he, too, expects Jefferson to treat him like a son. Harriet believes that knowing the truth will make her strong. Knowing who she is will help Harriet hold on to her true identity.

Harriet fears that her identity as Harriet Hemings will be totally erased. She tells her mother, "You won't let them say, when I go, that there never was a Harriet" (*Wolf*, 241). Beverly has already told Harriet that she does not exist in Jefferson's written records, except as a slave. Beverly says, "On bread lists. On blanket lists. We're on those lists. . . . With all his other slaves. . . . Mama's there, too. Just like we're on the lists for the shirts he gave out, and the hats and the woolens. . . . We're slaves to him, Harriet. Nothing more" (*Wolf*, 211–212). Harriet, who looks up to Jefferson as a father, is officially just a slave. Harriet realizes, "We'd lived our lives here, and they had been good. But where it counted, where men wrote things down in their golden books that told about family, we were not" (*Wolf*, 213).

When Beverly tells Harriet about the lack of any kind of documentation, not one piece of paper, that would link Jefferson and his children by their slave mother, Harriet takes this information as a gift of courage. She realizes that Jefferson will never tell her the truth, that he uses "innocence as a weapon. Silence as a shield" (*Wolf*, 246). Harriet is ready to break the bonds that make her a slave, subject to Jefferson. As she leaves Monticello, Harriet tells Jefferson to write about her departure in his farm records, and she addresses Jefferson as "Mister," not Master, for the first time. This is her first act of independence. Jefferson is not giving her freedom; she is taking it. Harriet says, "Oh, inside me something was singing! I have done it. . . . I have called him Mister Jefferson! I have broken my bonds! I am free!" (*Wolf*, 247). Harriet Hemings is ready to forge her own unique identity; she will not let Jefferson or others define who she is. She chooses not to be the slave of Jefferson, but a person who makes her own way in the world.

CREATING YOUR OWN DESTINY

The same need to be free and to forge a unique identity faces Phillis Wheatley, the first African American poet in America, in *Hang a Thousand Trees with Ribbons* (1996). John Peters, the man who marries Phillis, sums up her conflict near the end of the novel. He says, "Your head is addled, Phillis. It isn't your fault. You're still struggling to figure if you're white or nigra. And now you don't know if you're British or American. It's time to decide."[1] Phillis responds, "Why must I be one thing or the other? I feel as if I am a part of many peoples" (*Ribbons*, 295). Phillis wants to be recognized as a poet and a person, but social barriers make this impossible in the eighteenth century.

Rinaldi used scholarly resources to create the biography of the early life of Wheatley, but, as in other historical novels, did not let the sources limit her. She "took risks with this book, in that I created my own Phillis, as I created my own Harriet in *Wolf by the Ears*" (*Ribbons*, 331–332). Rinaldi wants us to see Wheatley as a flesh and blood person with complex motives and needs. So she depicts Phillis as a confused teen, torn by the conflicting roles she was forced to live. Wheatley was "given the celebrity, the adulation . . . yet held on the tether of slavery" (*Ribbons*, 332). Because of her situation, Rinaldi believes that throughout her life, Phillis struggled with the question of her identity, just like Harriet Hemings.

The novel begins in 1772 when Phillis is seventeen and her patrons and owners, the Wheatleys, are trying to gather subscribers to get her first book of poems published. Phillis is going to be examined by "a committee of the most noble men in Boston" in order to prove that she has written her poems. To Phillis her writing lets her be "the real me . . . whole, beautiful, alive, filled with a sense of pleasure and worth" (*Ribbons*, 22). But the committee views Phillis's poetry as an important test case about the humanness of blacks. If Phillis has written the poems, then blacks are capable of producing art and are equal members of the human race. If Phillis is lying, then this is proof that blacks are incapable of creating art and "destined, forever, to be slaves" (*Ribbons*, 20). The "future of the race" rides on Phillis's shoulders. For Phillis this test case represents her identity crisis. She is a poet who writes poetry for the sheer love of the words, but people are often interested in her poetry because it represents an oddity, poetry written by a black woman. When she writes she is free, while in reality she is a slave.

Phillis was educated, in the first place, as an experiment by Nathaniel Wheatley, her master's son, to prove that a common person can be educated. Reading and writing do not make Phillis free. Nathaniel controls her studies and revises her letters. When she protests, he tells her, "Negroes shouldn't be taught to read and write, Phillis. And they have no rights under English law" (*Ribbons*, 119). Nathaniel also demands Phillis forget her past and give up African customs. Like Harriet Hemings, Phillis finds herself caught in "a velvet trap" of being cared for and yet controlled as a person without human rights.

Phillis writes, secretly, because it makes her feel free, but when she is twelve her poems are discovered, and from that day her writing belongs to the Wheatley family. She is identified as "Mrs. Wheatley's nigra girl who writes poetry" (*Ribbons*, 146). Again and again Phillis is asked to put aside her true feelings as a black woman and slave. She is asked to recite to a slave trader, to be portrayed as a servant in order to get her poems published, to prove herself to the learned men of the colonies. But Phillis is never seen as an equal person. She realizes that people look at her as "a thing, an oddment, like a bear brought here by a sea captain and displayed on a chain on the wharf" (*Ribbons*, 159).

Black friends, both slave and free, warn Phillis that nothing matters, no fame is sufficient, if she isn't free. When she travels to London with Nathaniel to publish her book of poems, Phillis meets people who encourage her to seek freedom. Benjamin Franklin sums up her situation, "Toasted here in London, and at home in bondage" (*Ribbons*, 244). With Franklin's encouragement, Phillis finally has the courage to demand her freedom, although she continues to serve her old master and mistress when she returns to Boston. Phillis realizes her dilemma: "They've treated me white. I've trusted their soft words. I've been coddled by everyone. . . . So here I am now, come to a pretty pass—white on the inside, where nobody can see it, and nigra on the outside, where it's all anybody sees" (*Ribbons*, 281-282).

Phillis struggles with this conflict of accepting herself as a black woman and making her own way as a poet while the colonies prepare to break away from Britain. She asks herself, "*Who will care about the poems of a little nigra girl if there is a war?*" and feels "*discarded, of no more use to anyone*" (*Ribbons*, 282). But she continues to write poems, pleasing herself alone. When she publishes a letter about the hypocrisy of Christian ministers who have slaves, Phillis is finding her voice. She tells Nathaniel, "I am a free nigra woman. . . . I must do everything I can do to exist" (*Ribbons*, 302). She hopes to be "freed by the fruits of my pen" (*Ribbons*, 302). Phillis achieves this sense of personal freedom when she meets George Washington, who treats her as an equal. Phillis writes a poem praising Washington and is invited to his headquarters. When he meets her, Washington addresses Phillis as "miss," a way in which no black woman was ever addressed. This recognition is powerful for Phillis. She says, "I felt things falling into place inside me. And for the first time in a long while everything seemed of a piece. I was whole for the first time in my life" (*Ribbons*, 317).

As they talk, Phillis and Washington realize they both lost their fathers when they were young, but Washington now considers this misfortune as an opportunity. He says, "It is up to us to find our destiny in our own way"

(*Ribbons*, 320). Phillis takes hope from his words for her own situation as a black woman, freed slave, and new American. She, like Harriet Hemings, comes to believe in herself and her courage to make sacrifices in order to "break new ground for those who follow" (*Ribbons*, 324).

ACCEPTING WHO YOU ARE

The idea for *Cast Two Shadows* (1998) came to Rinaldi when she was thinking about how a child of mixed racial background would feel if she met her black grandmother and got to know her.[2] Unlike Harriet, who doesn't know for sure if Jefferson is her father, or Phillis Wheatley, who lost her father when she was carried off by slavers, Caroline Whitaker, the main character in this story, knows her white father and her black grandmother, Miz Melindy. She doesn't know her black mother. This novel explores how Caroline grows up as she deals with her identities as a child of a black mother and white father and how she shapes this knowledge into her sense of herself.

Caroline is fourteen when the British arrive in Camden, South Carolina; hang her best friend, Kit Gales; imprison her father, who is a rebel leader; and place the rest of her family under house arrest while the British ravage their plantation. Rinaldi shows how the Revolutionary War in the South became a civil war, with "families taking different sides. Neighbor fighting against neighbor" (*Shadows*, 57) and people changing sides as they dealt with the British soldiers. Johnny, Caroline's older brother, chooses to fight as a Loyalist until he sees how the British have no compunction about trampling on his rights. He is whipped because he refuses to give his prize horse to a British officer. Rinaldi based her portrait of the Whitaker family on the family of Joseph Kershaw, Camden's founding father, but created the characters of the wife and children and Miz Melindy, "the black grandmother of a child who dwelt in the plantation house" (*Shadows*, 273–274, 276).

Caroline knows she lived with Miz Melindy until she was two and that she was taken to "the big house" only when "some casual visitors came by and thought Mama Sarah had had another baby" (Shadows, 35). She also knows there is "bad blood" between her family and Miz Melindy's family in the slave quarters that neither family will talk about. Caroline says, "We go out of our way not to speak of it. We walk around it" (*Shadows*, 24). Miz Melindy will have nothing to do with Caroline either; instead, "she will chase me and pretend she never laid eyes on me before" (Shadows, 23). Even so Caroline accepts herself. She says, "I was used to being an embarrassment to people. My whole past, far as I could remember, was spoken about in whispers, when spoken of at all" (*Shadows*, 30–31). She remembers clearly when she was four and Johnny, her older brother, told her she was different from other people, that she "cast two shadows" instead of one. Johnny said, "You cast two, because your real mama, who died, was part negra" (*Shadows*, 37). Now at fourteen she knows that her family is in a "pretty mess" with all the confusing relationships and hurtful events that have occurred between blacks and whites.

But Caroline doesn't know her complete history. When Johnny deserts the British army and sends for help, she journeys with her grandmother, Miz Melindy, to rescue him. Now Caroline has the chance to ask the questions that trouble her. She says, "I wasn't going to make a two-day journey with her sitting right next to me on that seat and not know how she felt about me" (*Shadows*, 98). Caroline has often wondered about why Miz Melindy hated her father when "he did no more with your daughter than you did with Mr. Bone" (*Shadows*, 99). Miz Melindy and Mr. Bone, the white overseer, are the parents of Caroline's mother.

On this journey Caroline also decides that she won't lie about Miz Melindy's identity as her grandmother anymore. She says, "There had been too much lying, about everything, in my life anyway" (*Shadows*, 103). Caroline feels this is a turning point for her; she is ready to learn the truth about who she is. But the people they meet don't believe Caroline, and Miz Melindy accuses her of being just as stubborn as her real mother. Suddenly, Caroline realizes her real mother is still alive, and that "the price for my being a part of the family was that my mother was sold off" (*Shadows*, 125). All the undercurrents at her home make sense. She thinks, "The world was falling back into place, starting to make sense to me" (*Shadows*, 124).

Several people give her advice about how to deal with the painful truth. Mrs. McClure, a woman who fears they might be spies and imprisons them for a night, tells Caroline she has to learn when to tell other people about her black grandmother and when to let it go. In other words, she has to balance her need to tell about herself with her need to accomplish her goals. Miz Melindy believes in perseverance. Her painful life experiences have taught her how to deal with pain. She says, "You set yerself to the task. You take a turn an' set yer heart to look in other ways" (*Shadows*, 136). Johnny tells Caroline that coping with her knowledge is part of being grown up. He says, "You have to stop thinking of how you feel about it. . . . Means you have to start to know that sometimes bad things happen in families. . . . And it takes time for people to get shut of their feelings about them" (*Shadows*, 159).

Caroline feels confused but tries to go on doing the best she can, using what she learns, making the experiences part of who she is. Her resolve is tested when she has to choose between allowing the whipping of one of the slaves or turning over her prize horse to the British. Caroline decides what she must do, in part because of her connection to Miz Melindy and the other blacks. But she also acts as she does because it is the right thing, the human thing to do. Caroline thinks, "A horse for a negra. Because I was half negra. And blood will out. . . . No, I thought. A horse for a human being. Because I was a human being" (*Shadows*, 248). Caroline's sense of herself expands beyond the limits of black or white, daughter of a white woman or a black woman. She identifies herself as a person who treats other people with compassion. Earlier Miz Melindy tried to teach her this important truth. She told Caroline, "The river give us all life . . . Flows by an' we all part of it. But the river doan know what it be, either. Up north it be the Catawba. Here it be the Wateree. Below us, where it runs itself into the ocean, it be the Santee. It be the river" (*Shadows*, 191). In the end Caroline understands that Miz Melindy was talking about the unity of all humans.

EXPLORING WHO YOU CAN BE

Rebecca Galloway's identity crisis in *The Second Bend in the River* (1997) resembles the choices faced by Harriet Hemings and Phillis Wheatley to live as a member of a particular culture. She has to choose either to live as a white woman or to become the wife of Chief Tecumseh of the Shawnees and adopt Indian culture. The novel covers a ten-year period from 1798 to 1808 when Rebecca meets and falls in love with Tecumseh. Rinaldi bases her story on extensive research about the Galloway family of Greene County, Ohio, although the romance between Rebecca and Tecumseh "is up for conjecture."[3] Finding "more evidence that it happened than evidence to dispute it" (*River*, 269), Rinaldi chose to explore the conflict within Rebecca of choosing between two different identities.

Rebecca, at seven, instinctively sees herself as different from Tecumseh. Even though she is so young, Rebecca measures Tecumseh's behavior against her way of life. She is frightened when she first sees him, but her father tells her Tecumseh is "civilized, friendly," a man of honor who has promised peace. Tecumseh visits the farmstead, not to threaten her family, but because it brings back memories of his childhood village. Rebecca is surprised when Tecumseh prays before he eats, or that he uses silverware, "properlike." She identifies him with a red-tailed hawk and as a part of nature. When she first sees him, "He seemed part of the trees, the undergrowth. Part of the landscape. Even part of the river and the sky. Like he belonged there" (*River*, 3).

She, on the other hand, identifies herself with books—"Books were all I had out there in the wilderness" (*River*, 5)—and cats, domestic animals "for people who are settled and civilized" (*River*, 11). Rebecca and her family have set out to "improve" the wilderness, to claim the land and work it as a farm, whereas Tecumseh is "something wild. Something forgotten" (*River*, 12).

At the same time, Rebecca feels attracted to the natural world that Tecumseh represents. She says, "*Our life was strange*, a mixture of civilized and savage" (*River*, 32). Rebecca is fascinated by white people who have chosen to live as Indians, Molly Kiser and Blue Jacket (Marmaduke Van Swearingen), but she also fears the wild; a part of her agrees with Phemy, a young girl who journeys to their settlement but refuses to stay because it is wild and "savage."

While Rebecca is growing up, Tecumseh continues to visit their farm and she learns that he is trying to "teach his people to be different" (*River*, 110). He is trying on the ways of civilization. He wants to fight whites with words, their own weapons. Tecumseh tells Rebecca, "Tecumseh has decided not to be a warrior with guns and war clubs. . . . Tecumseh has decided to be a warrior with words. . . . if all Indians unite like the Shemanese, they will have to negotiate with us in an honorable way" (*River*, 107). Rebecca teaches Tecumseh to improve his reading and use of English and so put on the ways of civilization.

At fourteen, Rebecca is attracted to Tecumseh, both for his physical grace as well his approach to the natural world. Rebecca says, "Then I'd lose myself in the world as he showed it to me from the canoe. He pointed out the tracks of animals, vegetation, I'd never paid mind to, herbs that his people used as medicine, fall flowers. . . . I had the feeling that he had told these things to no white before. That I was being honored" (*River*, 168–169). When Rebecca is sixteen, Tecumseh asks for her hand in marriage, and she faces a choice between two ways of life. Rebecca says, "I was flooded with a warm feeling of completeness, of knowing I would never be unsure of anything again. It lasted only a minute. Then I thought. *Marry him?* Go and live in an Indian village?" (*River*, 241). After struggling with herself, Rebecca decides she must "live as a white woman. I need my children raised as whites" (*River*, 254). She loves Tecumseh but has become too civilized, while she continues to see Tecumseh as she first saw him, a part of nature.

In Rebecca's struggle and choice, Rinaldi shows the deep attraction of different identities, how adolescents try out these identities, and how they often choose to define themselves in one way. Rinaldi also suggests in the meeting of Rebecca Galloway and Tecumseh how in the nineteenth century the cultural differences between Native Americans and whites could seem insurmountable to both and ultimately lead to conflict when people saw themselves as essentially different from each other. Rebecca and Tecumseh love each other and value the other's culture even though they decide they cannot give up their different ways of life to live together. Rinaldi leaves the reader wondering what would have happened for Native American and white relations if either one had made a different decision.

CHOOSING A NEW SELF

In several novels, Rinaldi uses the father-daughter relationship to explore how young women shape their own identity by either accepting or rejecting their father's worldview. In the novel, *In My Father's House* (1993), Rinaldi uses events in the lives of Wilmer McLean and his family, focusing on McLean's relationship with his stepdaughter, Oscie Mason. The Battle of Manassas, the first major battle of the war, started at the McLean family plantation in Northern Virginia, and the treaty that ended the war was signed in the parlor of McLean's home in Appomattox, Virginia. This historic fact gives Rinaldi a unique opportunity to examine the motivation and changes that occurred in these family members from the beginning to the end of the Civil War. Rinaldi chronicles events from 1851 to 1865 through the eyes of Oscie Mason as she grows from a child of seven to a young woman of twenty. Oscie has to choose between two different ways of life, the Old South or the New South, which are embodied in two dominant men in Oscie's life, her father, Doctor John, and her stepfather, Will McLean. Rinaldi suggests why McLean changes "from a staunch patriot to a man who speculated in sugar, making money on the war" (*House*, 309) and how Oscie changes as she rejects and then accepts her stepfather. As she grows from the child of her birth-father to the child of her stepfather, Oscie creates her own identity.

Even at seven Oscie Mason realizes the fundamental differences between her father, who is dead, and her new stepfather. Doctor John "blended in." He represented tradition and the time-honored way of doing things. He realized slavery was wrong, but he kept slaves, as his family always had. He treated the slaves like family, and he protected and took care of everyone on the plantation, especially his wife and children. Will McLean, on the other hand, "stuck out on the landscape. . . . He brought some of the outside world with him, something that did not belong" (*House*, 6). While also raised in the South, McLean hates the slave system and has never bought a slave. He has abolitionist leanings. He is also a realist; he sees the world is changing because of industrialization and the lopsided balance of trade between the North and the South. As a merchant, he knows that the South is in a bad situation. He considers himself different from Oscie's father, even though he doesn't always know what this means. He tells Oscie, "He was Old South. I'm New South" (*House*, 63).

Oscie was deeply attached to her father and charged by him to take care of the family. She resents McLean's interference as she tries to be strong and follow in his footsteps. Oscie likes the way things are and wants most of all to be like her mother. McLean, however, hires a Yankee tutor, Elvira Buttonworth, to teach Oscie and her sisters to think for themselves. McLean also treats the slaves differently. He refuses to sell a slave, Mary Ann, when Oscie hears gossip that she is a witch. Even when she sees the scars Mary Ann carries from being whipped by her former master, Oscie defends the Southern way of treating the slaves. After the death of Oscie's little sister, Mary Ann is blamed and banished from the house to work as a field hand. Oscie knows Mary Ann is pregnant but doesn't tell McLean; she is just happy to see her go. Later she refuses to accept responsibility when Mary Ann loses her baby due to harsh working conditions and her lack of physical stamina. She thinks slaves are supposed to be able to take this treatment and have to be treated this way to keep them in line.

As she grows up, Oscie knows the world is changing but thinks that their lives on the plantation are protected from politics. However, in 1860 her tutor is forced to leave because of strong anti-Northern sentiment, and Oscie's childhood ends. Before the first battle of the Civil War, which takes place on their plantation, near Manassas junction, Oscie meets Captain Alexander, a Confederate officer, married man and distant relative. Oscie sees in him the embodiment of the Southern way. Alexander is committed to the South and his honor as a Southern gentleman. So even though he does not believe in secession and knows the South has little chance of winning, he enlists in the Confederate Army. He could have stayed out West and had a successful career, but he chose honor and duty before his own needs. Oscie realizes that he would risk his life even though he doesn't believe in the Southern Cause. His sense of honor is the way of the Old South. Part of Oscie's attraction to Alexander has to do with her need to hold on to the past for awhile. But in the end, Oscie sees the limits of the ways of the Old South. She thinks, "What good will all that honor do you on the battlefield. It can't take the place of the men and equipment the Yankees have" (*House*, 152). Oscie understands what McLean meant about how the South needs to examine what it stands for. What does it mean to be a Southerner and what are they fighting for? When Oscie leaves her father's plantation, her father's house, and says good-bye to Alexander, she knows "Our life was finished here" (*House*, 154). She has "no more romantic notions about the South" (*House*, 170).

Oscie's realization causes her to identify with McLean. She understands that he needs to make a new life for the family, based on a new sense of reality. She defends Will to her sister and to her mother. She tells McLean, "I see the future of the South when I look at you. . . . It isn't the future Alex saw. All that sweet tradition. You're brash . . . But you know about real things none of us have had to face before. I think you're all about what the South is going to have to be if we want to stay alive" (*House*, 181). Oscie respects his willingness to change and fight to forge a new life for his family.

Oscie, also, faces the impact of slavery on the Old South. She wants to blame the slave Mary Ann for making trouble, especially when Mary Ann tells McLean that there was gossip about Oscie's relationship with Alexander. Oscie feels angry and guilty. She thinks that Mary Ann has "been a shadow hanging over the place. Trouble." But then she is "overcome with guilt, pondering on Mary Ann's lost babies, knowing I was to blame" (*House*, 144–145). McLean challenges Oscie to recognize what is really going on. He says, "She's what this slavery business is all about. Her fate being all tied in with ours. People owning people, buying them, selling them, inheriting them. . . . What Mary Ann became isn't her fault, but the fault of others who had power over her" (*House*, 147). Oscie doesn't immediately recognize the truth of what McLean is telling her, but when Mary Ann protects her from townspeople who are angry over McLean's speculating, Oscie admits to herself and Mary Ann how she abused her power. When Mary Ann says, "We both done mean things to each other," Oscie responds, "I was supposed to know better" (*House*, 220). Oscie realizes the evils of the slave system that gives one person control over another. She apologizes to Mary Ann: "When you came . . . I had so many fears. I was still missing my daddy. . . . I took everything out on you" (*House*, 221). She also helps Mary Ann secure her freedom.

Giving up her romantic notions about the South and realizing the evils of slavery cause Oscie to change. She gives up her identity with her father and the Old South and identifies with Will McLean. She knows the past is gone and no one is the same as they were before the war. She sees McLean as the father of her new self, a person with a new realistic vision and energy to do what has to be done to build the future.

EMERGING AS A WHOLE PERSON

In *Mine Eyes Have Seen* (1998), one of Rinaldi's most recent novels, the focus is also on the father-daughter relationship of Annie Brown and her father, John Brown. Annie Brown tells the story of John Brown's Provisional Army and the summer they spent at the Kennedy Farm in the foothills of western

Maryland, planning the raid on the arsenal at Harper's Ferry. Rinaldi says in her note to the novel, "We know what people did and when, but not why. We are not privy to their private emotions, fears, hopes, or wishes. So historical writers must create and fill in the gaps" (*Eyes*, 267). Rinaldi uses this opening to examine how Annie felt about her father and what being John Brown's daughter meant to Annie's identity. Like Harriet in *Wolf by the Ears*, Annie has an ambivalent reaction to her father. And like Jefferson, Brown refuses to deal directly with his daughter's deepest need. Annie, at fifteen, believes that Brown blames her for the death of her baby sister, Amelia, who died from burns in a household accident when Annie was three. Until she knows if he blames her, Annie cannot resolve her guilt or become independent to form her own identity.

Jefferson uses silence and kindness to deflect Harriet's need to learn the identity of her father, while Brown puts Annie off with his authoritarian behavior. Annie says, "I'm that 'strange Annie' to him. We don't get on" (*Eyes*, 13). But most people find Brown a difficult man. Annie says, "People loved him and hated him. It confused you so. It made your soul all twisted up inside like a snake" (*Eyes*, 15–16). Brown is single-mindedly dedicated to the antislavery movement. Slavery, to him, was "like original sin. We either commit it or inherit it" (*Eyes*, 8), and it required "blood atonement." Annie says, "We'd known all of our lives that Pa was going to do armed resistance against slavery. The knowledge had grown in us, along with our sinew and bones" (*Eyes*, 7). Everything else takes second place to this commitment. Jason, one of Annie's brothers, warns her that their father is a hard man. He says, "He uses people. . . . He goes through them. And like everyone who uses people, he can conjure up all the charm when he wants" (*Eyes*, 22).

At first Annie feels special that her father needs her at the Kennedy Farm where he is assembling his Provisional Army. But then she realizes that he wants her to be the lookout and do whatever it takes to keep strangers away from the house, even lie. Annie says, "I understood. I was to do what Pa considered most despicable. Oh daughter of troops. I was to lie" (*Eyes*, 54). Annie, however, hoping to make up to Brown for her sister's death, is willing to do whatever it takes "to get Pa to love me" (*Eyes*, 66). She waits for him to speak to her. She says, "I waited, holding my breath, for him to say something now about this thing that lay between us. But there was no bringing him around" (*Eyes*, 82).

Annie only begins to deal with her guilt with the help of a neighbor, Mrs. Huffmaster, who can heal people, read auras, and conjure up the dead. Mrs. Huffmaster sees immediately that Annie's spirit is troubled. She asks her, "Who you got on the other side that you need forgivin' from" (*Eyes*,

85). For the first time, Annie confides her guilt and her belief that her father has never forgiven her. But Mrs. Huffmaster says, "Never mind 'bout your pa. . . . You hafta forgive yourself! . . . You be yer own best friend. . . . You gots to forgive yerself. And be at peace. An' you gots to let Amelia go, so's she kin be at peace. Onliest way to do that is fer you to know that Amelia doan blame you fer what happened" (*Eyes*, 87–88). When Mrs. Huffmaster contacts her dead sister, Annie feels "a lightness inside me, as if my own soul were rising, lifting, upward too. . . . I felt her presence, standing there. *I knew she was with me.* And I knew, too, that she forgave me and that it didn't matter if Pa did not" (*Eyes*, 91).

After this experience, Annie feels good about herself, even though her father doesn't change. At first Annie is angry, but that only creates more guilt. Instead Annie decides to help her father, having no expectations that he will change. When the men are trying to decide whether to stand with Brown in the raid, Annie helps. She gets Dangerfield Newby, a former slave, to share a letter from his wife in which she begs Newby to buy her and their seven children before they are sold down South. Annie knows that if Brown's men hear this, they'll support Brown. The letter works and Annie knows that she has had a part in their decision. She thinks, "I'd live with it for the rest of my life. And that is as real as it gets" (*Eyes*, 149). She also helps her father find a sign from the Lord about what he should do, even though she fears he mistakes her for the dead Amelia.

When Brown tries to dismiss Annie at the end, she has the courage to ask for his forgiveness, to settle this thing between them. Annie is left with the stern reality of knowing her father could never forgive her. She realizes that she cannot expect him to change. Only she can accept herself and go on with her life. Again, Mrs. Huffmaster helps her to see this important truth. She says, "The 'portant thing . . . is that you done yer best. You done what you wuz brung here to do" (*Eyes*, 231). Annie, like Harriet, achieves insight into her father's character, which gives her the independence to stop looking to him for approval. She begins to develop a sense of herself as an independent person.

Each of these adolescent girls has answered the question: Who am I? Harriet Hemings and Caroline Whitaker struggle with limited knowledge, while Phillis Wheatley feels controlled by others' conception of her identity. Rebecca Galloway chooses, not without regret, between two different possibilities, and Annie Brown and Oscie McLean look to their fathers, accepting or rejecting the ways of life represented by their behavior. Their choices aren't clear-cut, nor are they final. Rinaldi gives us a sense in each of these novels that the characters are reaching resolutions that will lead to growth as they continually make the choices that define who they are.

• *Afterword* •

Bringing History to Life

Since the early 1980s Rinaldi has created an impressive body of young adult historical fiction. In her novels, Rinaldi creates characters whose voices and points of view draw readers into a particular social and historical milieu, enabling readers to experience the feelings of people living in the period. This gives readers a unique perspective, since they already know the outcome. But for the moment they can feel what it must have been like to be a part of events, without knowing their full implications. This dynamic enlivens the study of history and enables readers to recognize the complexities of historical events.

Rinaldi is a master storyteller. Her novels are engaging not only as historical studies but also because they bring to life well-rounded and psychologically interesting characters. Rinaldi creates young women who are coming of age in the midst of political and social events that mirror their personal development. Whether it is the period of the Salem witch trials, the Revolutionary War, or the 1940s, the conflicts faced in society at a particular historic moment are mirrored by the psychological conflicts faced by the heroine. By learning the difference between appearance and reality, making moral choices, and becoming independent, the heroines forge their personal identities.

Rinaldi continues to explore these themes in her two latest novels, *Amelia's War* and *The Coffin Quilt* (both published in 1999). *Amelia's War* shows the impact of the war on the civilians in Hagerstown, Maryland. Divided loyalties turn neighbor against neighbor, beginning with the murder of Dewitt Clinton Rench, a young man who joins the Confederate Army and is gunned down in his hometown. The editor of the local newspaper, arrested for "Southern leanings," is sent to prison. Citizens watch for the colors of the advancing army and flee the town, depending on their loyalties.

81

In 1864, Confederate Brigadier General John McCausland demands two hundred thousand dollars from the town and clothing for the soldiers. If the town fails to meet the "ransom," it will be burned to the ground. Somehow, the figure on the order given to the town's officials is changed to twenty thousand dollars, an amount the town can pay, and it is saved. In this story, Rinaldi has Amelia making the crucial change in the orders. This is an important personal decision for her. After trying not to take sides, not to get involved in the conflicts that turn her neighbors against each other, Amelia realizes that she must make a choice. In the end, she shows courage and commitment.

The Coffin Quilt recounts the infamous feud between the Hatfields and McCoys, told from the point of view of the youngest daughter of the McCoy family, Fanny. Fanny recollects events going back to 1880, when she was seven and her sister Roseanna ran off with Johnse Hatfield without getting married. This act brings to a boil bad feelings that have simmered between the families since the Civil War.

Loving her sister deeply, Fanny defends her to others and even goes with her when she warns the Hatfields that her lover Johnse has been arrested. Roseanna's betrayal of her family severs her ties with them, and they are drawn deeper into killing and revenge. Fanny begins to question her sister's motives, however, and realizes that Roseanna has a self-destructive urge, which has touched them all. Fanny decides not to aid Roseanna anymore, not to give her a letter from her lover that could only prolong the suffering and killing. Fanny's growth in understanding and courage helps her make the difficult choice between her sister and the family's need for healing. In this way Fanny matures. This is a pattern that Rinaldi has explored with many of her adolescent characters.

Rinaldi has created an impressive cast of female protagonists, who, like most adolescent characters, are coming of age in worlds they question or even find unsupportive and threatening. In a gentle but clear way, Rinaldi questions gender expectations and shows that each person has potential that goes far beyond social expectations. The struggles of Rinaldi's characters, their growth, and their reintegration into the community with the knowledge they have gained about themselves can be instructive for young readers, especially young women.

Rinaldi is proud to be a "leading writer of historicals for young people in America." She believes that "something was given to me by the different experiences in my life." This has helped her create her novels. She wants to continue to write to make history come to life for young adults, and she has "lots of ideas." She promises to continue to write history to inspire and motivate young people.

Notes

CHAPTER 1. BECOMING A WRITER OF HISTORICAL FICTION

1. Metropolitan Museum of Art, New York City.

2. The quotations attributed to Rinaldi in this chapter, and throughout the book, are primarily from an interview conducted by the author on June 22, 1998, at Rinaldi's home in Somerville, New Jersey. Additional information came from subsequent telephone interviews. This interview is also usually the source of biographical details. Additional quotes are cited from *Something about the Author* (Gale Research, 1988), volume 51 and (Gale Research, 1994), volume 78; hereafter cited in text as *SATA*.

3. *Broken Days* (Scholastic, 1995), viii. Hereafter cited in text as *Days*.

4. *In My Father's House* (Scholastic, 1993), 311. Hereafter cited in text as *House*.

5. L.H. Butterfield, Marc Friedlaender, and Mary Jo Kline, eds., *The Book of Abigail and John: Selected Letters of the Adams Family, 1762–1784* (Harvard University Press, 1975).

6. *The Fifth of March* (Harcourt Brace Jovanovich, 1992), 326–327. Hereafter cited in text as *March*.

7. *A Ride into the Morning* (Harcourt Brace Jovanovich, 1991), 279. Hereafter cited in text as *Morning*.

8. *My Heart Is on the Ground* (Scholastic, 1999), 196. Hereafter cited in text as *Heart*.

9. "Primary Sources" <http://home.epix.net/~landis/primary.html> (p. 2).

10. Marlene Atleo, Naomi Caldwell, Barbara Landis, Jean Mendoza, Deborah Miranda, Debbie Reese, LaVera Rose, Beverly Slapin, and Cynthia Smith, "*My Heart Is on the Ground* and the Boarding School Experience" *Multicultural Review* (September 1999), vol. 8, 41–46.

11. <http://www.oyate.org/avoid.htm> (p. 14). Hereafter referred to as *Oyate* in the text.

12. April 1, 1999, vol. 95, 1428.

13. February 1, 1999, vol. 67, 228.

14. *Mine Eyes Have Seen* (Scholastic, 1998), iii. Hereafter cited in text as *Eyes*.

15. *The Last Silk Dress* (Holiday House, 1988), xiii. Hereafter cited in text as *Dress*.

16. *Finishing Becca* (Harcourt Brace, 1994), 345. Hereafter cited in text as *Becca*.
17. *A Stitch in Time* (Scholastic, 1994), 301. Hereafter cited in text as *Stitch*.
18. *The Blue Door* (Scholastic, 1996), 266. Hereafter cited in text as *Blue Door*.
19. "Carlisle Indian Industrial School History" <http://home.epix.net/~landis/histry.html> (p. 3).
20. See Nina Linday's summary of this discussion on March 12, 1999, at the Child_Lit site <http://www.scils.rutgers.edu/childlit/march99/0220.html>

CHAPTER 2. FROM JOURNALIST TO FICTION WRITER

1. *Wolf by the Ears* (Scholastic, 1991), x. Hereafter cited in text as *Wolf*.
2. *Keep Smiling Through* (Harcourt Brace, 1996), x. Hereafter cited in text as *Smiling*.
3. *Term Paper* (Walker, 1980), 1. Hereafter cited in text as *Term*.
4. *Library Journal* (October 1, 1980), vol. 105, 2122.
5. *Promises Are for Keeping* (Walker, 1982), 14. Hereafter cited in text as *Promises*.
6. *The Good Side of My Heart* (Holiday House, 1987), 9. Hereafter cited in text as *Good Side*.
7. *But in the Fall I'm Leaving* (Holiday House, 1985), 39. Hereafter cited in text as *Fall*.

CHAPTER 3. COMING OF AGE AS AMERICANS

1. *The Secret of Sarah Revere* (Harcourt Brace, 1995), 14. Hereafter cited in text as *Secret*.
2. *Time Enough for Drums* (Holiday House, 1986), 24. Hereafter cited in text as *Drums*.

CHAPTER 4. CONFRONTING CONFLICTING VALUES

1. *A Break with Charity* (Harcourt Brace Jovanovich, 1992), 31. Hereafter cited in text as *Charity*.
2. *An Acquaintance with Darkness* (Harcourt Brace, 1997), 4. Hereafter cited in text as *Darkness*.

CHAPTER 5. FORGING INDIVIDUAL IDENTITY

1. *Hang a Thousand Trees with Ribbons* (Harcourt Brace, 1996), 295. Hereafter cited in text as *Ribbons*.

2. *Cast Two Shadows* (Harcourt Brace, 1998), 277. Hereafter cited in text as *Shadows*.

3. *The Second Bend in the River* (Scholastic, 1997), 269. Hereafter cited in text as *River*.

Bibliography

NOVELS

An Acquaintance with Darkness. Harcourt Brace, 1997.

Amelia's War. New York: Scholastic, 1999.

The Blue Door. Vol. 3 "Quilt Trilogy." New York: Scholastic, 1996.

A Break with Charity: A Story about the Salem Witch Trials. New York: Harcourt Brace Jovanovich, 1992.

Broken Days. Vol. 2 "Quilt Trilogy." New York: Scholastic, 1995.

But in the Fall I'm Leaving. New York: Holiday House, 1985.

Cast Two Shadows: The American Revolution in the South. New York: Harcourt Brace, 1998.

The Coffin Quilt. New York: Harcourt Brace, 1999.

The Fifth of March: A Story of the Boston Massacre. New York: Harcourt Brace, 1993.

Finishing Becca: A Story about Peggy Shippen and Benedict Arnold. New York: Harcourt Brace, 1994.

The Good Side of My Heart. New York: Holiday House, 1987.

Hang a Thousand Trees with Ribbons: The Story of Phillis Wheatley. New York: Harcourt Brace, 1996.

In My Father's House. New York: Scholastic, 1993.

Keep Smiling Through. New York: Harcourt Brace, 1996.

The Last Silk Dress. New York: Holiday House, 1988.

Mine Eyes Have Seen. New York: Scholastic, 1998.

My Heart Is on the Ground: The Diary of Nannie Little Rose, a Sioux Girl. New York: Scholastic, 1999.

Promises Are for Keeping. New York: Walker, 1982.

A Ride into the Morning: The Story of Tempe Wick. New York: Harcourt Brace, 1991.

The Second Bend in the River. New York: Scholastic, 1997.

The Secret of Sarah Revere. New York: Harcourt Brace, 1995.

A Stitch in Time. Vol. 1 "Quilt Trilogy." New York: Scholastic, 1994.

Term Paper. New York: Walker, 1980.

Time Enough for Drums. New York: Holiday House, 1986.

Wolf by the Ears. New York: Scholastic, 1991.

INTERVIEWS

Dessau, D. Ilana, and Jenna Galley. "Interview with Ann Rinaldi." September 14, 1996. <http://www.scils.rutgers.edu/special/kay/rinaldi1.html>

ESSAYS OR ARTICLES

Commire, Anne, ed. *Something about the Author*, vol. 51, 149–151. Detroit: Gale Research, 1988.

Dessau, D. Ilana, and Jenna Galley with Professor Kay E. Vandergrift. "Learning about Ann Rinaldi." Created March 25, 1996; updated January 17, 1999. <http://www.scils.rutgers.edu/special/kay/rinaldi.html>

Hile, Kevin S., ed. *Something about the Author*, vol. 78, 169–173. Detroit: Gale Research, 1994.

McGregor, Joy H. "Ann Rinaldi." In *Writers for Young Adults*, edited by Ted Hipple, 75-85. New York: Charles Scribner's Sons, 1997.

SELECTED BOOK REVIEWS

An Acquaintance with Darkness
Publishers Weekly 244 (July 7, 1997): 69.
School Library Journal 43 (October 1997): 138.
Voice of Youth Advocates 16 (February 1998): 390.

The Blue Door
Book Report 15 (March 1997): 40.
Voice of Youth Advocates 19 (February 1997): 332.

A Break with Charity
Book Report 11 (January 1993): 48+.
Horn Book Magazine 68 (November 1992): 730.
Language Arts 70 (December 1993): 683.
Publishers Weekly 239 (August 3, 1992): 72.
School Library Journal 38 (September 1992): 279.
Voice of Youth Advocates 15 (December 1992): 285.

But in the Fall I'm Leaving
Blakely, Sherry D. *Voice of Youth Advocates* 8 (August 1985): 189.
Children's Book Review Service 13 (Spring 1985): 133.
Publishers Weekly 227 (June 7, 1985): 81.
Publishers Weekly 229 (June 27, 1986): 98.

School Library Journal 31 (August 1985): 80–81.
Social Education 50 (April 1986): 301.

The Fifth of March
Booklist 90 (January 15, 1994): 925.
Horn Book Guide 5 (Spring 1994): 90.
Kirkus Reviews 61 (December 1, 1993): 1528.
MacRae, Cathi Dunn. "The Young Adult Perplex." *Wilson Library Bulletin* 68 (May 1994): 100+.
Publishers Weekly 240 (November 8, 1993): 78.
School Library Journal 40 (January 1994): 132+.
Voice of Youth Advocates 16 (February 1994): 372.
Voice of Youth Advocates 18 (June 1995): 90.

Finishing Becca
Booklist 91 (November 15, 1994): 590+.
Book Report 14 (May/June 1995): 41.
Horn Book Guide 6 (Spring 1995): 90.
Kirkus Reviews 63 (December 15, 1994): 1575.
Language Arts 73 (February 1996): 146.

The Good Side of My Heart
English Journal 78 (April 1989): 88.
Journal of Reading 33 (November 1989): 115.
Publishers Weekly 231 (May 8, 1987): 72.
School Library Journal 33 (August 1987): 98.
Voice of Youth Advocates 10 (August 1987): 122.

Hang a Thousand Trees with Ribbons
Book Report 15 (March 1997): 40–41.
Reading Teacher 51 (November 1997): 244.

In My Father's House
Book Report 12 (September 1993): 48.
English Journal 83 (January 1994): 80.
Publishers Weekly 240 (April 26, 1993): 80.
Publishers Weekly 241 (November 21, 1994): 79.
School Library Journal 39 (March 1993): 224.
Voice of Youth Advocates 16 (June 1993): 94.
Keep Smiling Through
School Library Journal 42 (June 1996): 124.

The Last Silk Dress
Publishers Weekly 233 (May 20, 1988): 93.

School Library Journal 34 (May 1988): 112.
Voice of Youth Advocates 11 (December 1988): 241.

Mine Eyes Have Seen
Booklist 94 (February 15, 1998): 1000.
Book Report 16 (March 1998): 35.

My Heart Is on the Ground: The Diary of Nannie Little Rose, a Sioux Girl
Booklist 95 (April 1, 1999): 1428.
"Books to Avoid: A Critical Review of Ann Rinaldi's *My Heart Is on the Ground. . . .*"
     <http://www.oyate.org/avoid.htm>
Kirkus Reviews 67 (February 1, 1999): 228.
Marlene Atleo, Naomi Caldwell, Barbara Landis, Jean Mendoza, Deborah Miranda,
     Debbie Reese, LaVera Rose, Beverly Slapin, and Cynthia Smith, "*My Heart Is
     on the Ground* and the Boarding School Experience." *Multicultural Review* 8
     (September 1999): 41–46.

Promises Are for Keeping
Chelton, Mary K. *Voice of Youth Advocates* 5 (August 1982): 36.
School Library Journal 28 (April 1982): 84.

A Ride into the Morning
Booklist 87 (August 1991): 2141.
Horn Book Guide 2 (Fall 1991): 278.
School Library Journal 37 (May 1991): 113.
Voice of Youth Advocates 14 (June 1991): 101.

The Second Bend in the River
Book Report 16 (May 1997): 36–37.
School Library Journal 43 (June 1997): 126.

The Secret of Sarah Revere
Booklist (November 15, 1995): 548.
Book Report 15 (May/June 1996): 39.

A Stitch in Time
Book Report 13 (September 1994): 44+.
School Library Journal 40 (March 1, 1994): 309.
Voice of Youth Advocates 17 (April 1994): 30.

Term Paper
Children's Book Review Service 9 (Winter 1991): 49.
Hart, Anna Biagioni. *School Library Journal* 27 (January 1981): 72.
Library Journal (October 1, 1980): 2122.

Publishers Weekly 218 (October 31, 1980): 86.

Time Enough for Drums
Children's Book Review Service 14 (August 1986): 157.
Publisher's Weekly 229 (May 30, 1986): 69.
School Library Journal 32 (May 1986): 108.
Kirkus Reviews 54 (April 1, 1986): 552.

Wolf by the Ears
Publishers Weekly 240 (January 4, 1993): 74.
School Library Journal 38 (June 1992): 51+.
Voice of Youth Advocates 14 (June 1991): 101.

Index

Acquaintance with Darkness, An 61–64
Adams, Abigail, 48, 50–52
Adams, John, 4, 50, 51
Amelia's War, 81–82

Blue Door, The, 12, 13–14
Break with Charity, A, 56–59
Broken Days, 11, 12, 13
Brown, John, 8, 77–79
But in the Fall I'm Leaving, 28–29,
    32–33, 34–35, 36

Carlisle Indian Industrial School, 6, 8,
    14, 16, 17
Cast Two Shadows, 71–73
Childhood of Rinaldi, 21–23
Coffin Quilt, The, 4, 81, 82
Cohen, Barbara, 24
Coming of age, 39–40, 53, 65

Erdrich, Louise, 8

Female characters, 9
Fifth of March, The, 18, 50–52
Finishing Becca, 10, 46–47, 48

Good Side of My Heart, The, 29, 33, 35,
    36–38

Hang a Thousand Trees with Ribbons,
    68–71

Hemings, Harriet, 5, 66–68, 78
Historical research, ix, 4–10
Historical site visits, 7–8, 16
Hyde, George, 17

Indian school newspapers, 6
In My Father's House, 3, 7, 9,
    75–77

Jefferson, Thomas, 5, 66–68, 78
Journalism career, 23–24

Keep Smiling Through, ix, x, 22, 39,
    59–61

Last Silk Dress, The, 10, 54–56, 64
Leutze, Emanuel, 1
Lindbergh baby, 5, 65

Marsh, Rachel, 4, 50–52
Mine Eyes Have Seen, 8, 77–79
My Heart Is on the Ground, 6–7, 8,
    14–18

Oyate, 7, 8, 16–18

Pratt, Richard Henry, 6, 8, 14
Promises Are for Keeping, 26–28,
    31–32

Quilt Trilogy, 10–14

Reenactments, 2–3
Reese, Debbie, 7, 8, 16, 18
Ride into the Morning, A, 7, 48–50
Rinaldi, Ron, Jr., 1, 2, 9

Second Bend in the River, The 73–75
Secret of Sarah Revere, The, 41–44
Shippen, Peggy, 10, 46–47, 48
Slaboda, Emil, 1
Somerset Messenger Gazette, 23
Stitch in Time, A, 11, 12–13

Tecumseh, 73–75
Term Paper, 25–26, 30–31, 34, 35–36, 38
Time Enough for Drums, x, 3, 44–46
Trentonian, 1, 3, 5, 23, 24

Washington, George, 1
Wolf by the Ears, 5, 22, 65, 66–68, 78
Women in American history, 9

About the Author

Jeanne M. McGlinn is currently an associate professor of education at the University of North Carolina at Asheville, where she teaches children's and adolescent literature courses and supervises students preparing to teach English and language arts. She is the author of numerous reviews of adolescent literature for *Voice of Youth Advocates* and the *Alan Review*. She has been a coordinator for the Classroom Materials column in the *Journal of Adolescent and Adult Literacy* for the past two years and also writes reviews for this journal. She has written study guides of Shakespeare's plays, published by Penguin, and articles on multicultural literature and teaching language arts.